Trouble, Trials, and Trust

STEPHANIE KAUFFMAN

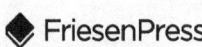

One Printers Way
Altona, MB, R0G 0B0
Canada

www.friesenpress.com

Copyright © 2022 by Stephanie Kauffman
First Edition — 2022

All rights reserved.

All Scripture quoted is in the King James Version.
To respect everyone's privacy, all names (including the author's) have been changed.

No part of this publication may be reproduced in any form, or by any means, electronic or mechanical, including photocopying, recording, or any information browsing, storage, or retrieval system, without permission in writing from FriesenPress.

ISBN
978-1-03-915683-8 (Hardcover)
978-1-03-915682-1 (Paperback)
978-1-03-915684-5 (eBook)

1. RELIGION, CHRISTIAN LIFE, WOMEN'S ISSUES

Distributed to the trade by The Ingram Book Company

FOREWORD AND DISCLAIMER

The world in which we live moves in a constant ebb and flow. Changes occur over time; things that were once acceptable no longer are, and vice versa. I don't endorse or recommend some of the actions taken in this book. This is simply my story of God's grace to me as I went through some difficult times in the early 1990s.

For people who have read my previous books to younger children, you may want to proofread chapters 15 to 22 and decide how much to leave in or skim read to young ones. I tried to present the reality I was living in without being too graphic.

DEDICATION

This book is dedicated Belinda, Javi, and his family. Thanks for seeing me through the rough and giving me the moments of joy.

I also dedicate it to Abbie and the Canmore family. Thanks for accepting me with all my foreign ways and ideas and making me such a part of your lives.

Your names have all been changed, but you and I know who you are. God bless!

Chapter 1

How can I live when my heart feels like it's breaking? How can I work when I couldn't care less? These were heavy thoughts for a twenty-four-year-old to ponder as I drove away from Manitoba, heading for a teaching position once again. Two days later on Friday, September 13, 1991, I pulled into Mayerthorpe, Alberta. We'd just finished burying my brother, Nick, in Ontario less than a month ago. Sitting around home crying wasn't going to help, but I could barely scrounge up the energy to feel like working, either. At least I was going back to a school where I'd previously taught. God had literally jolted me out of my apathy of not caring if I lived or died a few weeks previously when my brother's wife came to visit. It was just a week after Nick's funeral and the weather matched our spirits. During a thunderstorm one night, a bolt of lightning hit a huge tree, causing it to crash down onto the camper van we were in. A tiny spark of lightning seared through me at the same time that the force of the tree limb hitting us threw me out of bed, causing me to hit the floor. I sent an instant prayer upward.

Okay, Lord, I get it. I'm sorry I said I wished I could die! Now could you please stop this horrible tingling, like an electric fence, all through my arm?

My arm stopped tingling as everything went numb. I looked at my fingers but they wouldn't close in a fist. I couldn't even wiggle them.

Uhm, okay, Lord, I'm not sure this is exactly great, either.

God certainly has a sense of humour. This was exactly what I needed to help me realize that although life was going to hurt for a long time, I still wanted to be part of it.

Now as I sat in the driveway of Bert, the principal of the school where I'd be working, I was vacillating again.

Lord, how do I tell him my brother has died? But how do I not? I left here a year ago to travel overseas, so they know I'll have changed a lot. But I'm not sure I can teach without crying, so they've got to know why I'm a basket case.

Just do it, Stacy.

As I got out of the car, Bert and his wife, Joyce, met me.

"Oh, my, it's good to have you back with us again, Stacy." Joyce looked me over with a big smile. "Oh, do you ever look good. You've lost a bunch of weight since we last saw you."

"Yeah, well, having a brother get killed in a car accident will do that to you." Dead silence. *Oops, Lord. When you said 'just do it,' I guess I just really 'did' it.*

Well, that's certainly one way to break the news, my child.

"I'm sorry. I just didn't know how to tell you."

Bert cleared his throat. "How long ago?"

"About four weeks."

Both of them sighed. Bert continued. "That's why you sounded so strange on the phone, isn't it?"

"Yeah."

Joyce patted my arm. "Are you sure you're ready to get back to work already? We'd understand."

I flicked a tear off my cheek. "Well, sitting around doing nothing doesn't help, so teaching will help me take my mind off it—I hope."

Bert opened the car door and hauled out my suitcase. "Well, you're staying with us for the weekend. We have possible accommodations pending for you. Do you want me to let everyone know about your brother, or did you want to tell them yourself?"

I smiled shakily at him. "Please do it. I've been dreading having to say it over and over."

I spent Saturday at the school going through the files and records and seeing to it that everything would be ready for Monday morning. I was grateful for the work that kept my mind occupied.

Sunday after church I went to the Browns' for lunch. Ethan and April Brown had become my family away from home, so it was natural for me to head there. Bert hadn't had time to let everyone know about my brother's accident, so the

Browns weren't aware. As we sat at the table, April spoke up.

"Stacy, you've slimmed down so much since you were here a year ago. I bet you've lost twenty pounds."

I looked at my plate. "Twenty-five."

Their only daughter at home, and my soon-to-be student, Belinda, piped up. "Why are you looking so gloomy? That's great."

Once again I just blurted out the news. "Not when it's because your brother is dead." Man, did I ever know how to kill a dining room conversation.

April heaved a half-sigh, half-prayer. "Oh, dear God …"

The Browns' six-year-old grandson, Keith, broke the silence. "Really? How?"

"He fell asleep at the wheel, hit a culvert, and flipped his jeep."

Keith's eyes lit up. "A jeep? Cool? Could you still drive it, or was it really smashed?"

"K-E-I-T-H!" I don't know who yelled loudest, Ethan or April, but in a strange way, Keith's matter-of-factness was actually easier for me to deal with than people's sympathy.

"Don't worry," I said to the Browns before turning to Keith to answer his questions.

Late that afternoon, Bert called.

"Well, we've got a place lined up for you," he said. "There's a dental clinic here that has a full basement underneath. They're willing to rent to you on the condition that their staff can still use the kitchen and bathroom. If you're okay with them continuing to use that for their lunch area, then you'll have a really nice big space to yourself. There are two large rooms with a connecting door between them. That can be your bedroom and spare room and can be locked.

Joyce broke into his conversation. "We have a bed and dresser you can use. The common area already has a couch and chair for the dental staff, and we'll ask the church people to donate whatever they might have. You should be comfortable there this year, and it's only a few blocks from the church."

So that became my home away from home. I received enough furniture from various church and school families that I had a very nice setup and could have visitors over.

Another reason I gave thanks for a place of my own was just dealing with Nick's death. I could roam the "house" at night; I could cry, throw pillows, and do whatever I needed to ease my grief without worrying about disturbing others. No one knew how many sleepless nights I went through that year, although Bert did get involved in one episode.

The thing that helped me most was my music. With the church so close, and the school being in its basement, the church piano became my solace. I often walked down there at 1:00 a.m. Letting myself in with my school key and relocking after myself, I'd make my way to the auditorium in the dark and just sit and play until 4:00 or 5:00 a.m. I have no idea what songs I played. I just invented music that brought solace to my soul.

Although this music was soothing to me, I didn't realize what it was doing to one poor policeman who had night duties. In the middle of one night, Bert received a phone call.

"I hate ta' bother ya' so late, but I cain't take it no more," were the words that floated over the telephone wire after the policeman identified himself.

Bert groggily came awake. "What's the matter, officer?"

"I ain't Irish, I ain't superstitious, but your church is creepin' me out."

"What's wrong with our church?"

"You got a haint in there, and I ain't taking on no ghost for ya."

Bert chuckled. "Well, we believe in the Holy Ghost, but I think you're talking about something different?"

The man sniffed. "Ya better believe it. For weeks now, every night as I make my round past your church, the saddest, most haunting music I ever heard comes waftin' out o' that building. There's no car anywhere in sight. I check the doors; they're all firmly locked. It's pitch black inside the whole building, yet that pianer in there just keeps a'goin'. It's enough to spook anyone."

Bert told the man he'd drive in and check it out.

"Yer gonna' go in that building with the haint still in there? Better wait until daylight."

Since Bert had a suspicion what he might find, he wasn't too worried. Furthermore, he had a sense of humour and thought it might be fun to spook the spook. So he drove up with his lights off and carefully let himself in with his key. Pausing a moment to let his eyes adjust to the darkness, he carefully felt his way across the entrance and used his hand on the pew ends to guide himself up to the piano.

Meanwhile, I was sitting on the bench just giving a crashing crescendo to the end of one of my pieces when a hand clamped on my shoulder.

"Y-e-e-e-e-i-ii-i-k-sss!" Instinctively my arm flew back, and with power-driven adrenaline my elbow nailed the torso of this "thing" behind me.

Whoo-ooosh! I heard the air leave a human body and a crash. Before I could even process a thought, I'd whirled around on the piano bench, and my foot snapped out a line drive into a shinbone.

"Sto-o-p! Stacy, it's Bert," was all he could wheeze out.

"Bert? Bert, that's you? What are you doing out at this time of night?"

There was a pause while he gulped a bit more air. "Trying to catch a ghost. You're spooking the police officers." He groaned and I sensed him sitting up.

"I'm so sorry, Bert." A giggle slipped between my lips. "I guess the ghost caught you, eh? Why on earth did you just grab me like that?"

He managed to stand up as I heard his voice from above me. "I thought it would be funny. I forgot how fast you react."

Once we got outside, he offered me a lift back home. "Do you come here often at night, Stacy?"

"Yes, I do. I can't sleep anyway, and this helps me."

Bert pulled into the dental clinic. "Well, do you think you could come up with some flag or sign to leave on the door? That way when the police make their rounds, they'll know it's you inside and everything is okay."

I hopped out of the car. "Sure, I can do that. Say, I do hope I didn't hurt you too much."

He grinned. "I do steer wrestling at rodeos. I'll survive, but you do pack a good wallop." He departed and I went inside to make cocoa and calm down.

As the year went on, I continued to have my music nights when needed but found a glow-in-the-dark strip that I attached to the door handle whenever I was inside. Neither policemen nor Bert ever disturbed me again.

Chapter 2

Getting back to work was easier than I expected because the students all knew me. Changes had occurred amongst all of us. My biggest surprise was at the change in Molly in just one year. She had matured in amazing ways and approached me shortly after the start of school.

"Miss K, I'd like to do what Monica did the other year with you."

My eyes popped. "You want to memorize the book of Proverbs for convention?"

"Yep."

"Molly, that sounds great, but it's a huge task. Remember how you used to wait until the very last day to stumble through just the monthly scripture passage?"

"Yeah, well, now I want to do it, so I wondered if you'd memorize it with me."

I knew Molly was extremely determined, and if she was the one making that decision, then she'd probably do it.

"I'm willing to, with the same condition that I gave Monica when we memorized a whole book."

"What's that?"

"You can't quit unless I do." She grinned and stuck out her hand. I shook it, mentally giving myself a talking to.

Stacy, you're out of your mind to try and memorize scripture this year. You can't even remember where you put something five minutes after the fact.

My child, it'll give you something good to focus on. (God wasn't going to let me wimp out before I even started.)

I'm getting only a couple hours of sleep a night.

Memorizing during the sleepless hours will give you something to do.

I'm taking the geometry course so I can teach it to Belinda. Plus I have two girls doing algebra. I hate math, so I'm going to be stressed out.

Memorizing is easy for you, so that will give you something different to unstress your brain.

This year is going to be too hard. I can't do this.

I never said life would be easy, but I promised to be with you through it.

Okay, Lord. I'll do it.

When the school realized what Molly and I were going to do, they had a meeting. At the end they agreed to run fundraisers to send Molly and me to the International Student Convention, which was going to be held in Texas at the end of May. We were both thrilled and with that as the end goal, it gave us the umph to get those thirty-one chapters memorized. I set up a schedule, and with eight verses a day, five days a week, quoting a chapter at a time with three errors allowed per chapter, we managed to get it done just before the Regional Student Convention, which was held in Vanderhoof, British Columbia.

The fundraising projects were diverse and interesting. The whole school got involved, and even though the other students weren't going, they pitched in wholeheartedly. We held car washes, bake sales, attended a Dealer's Fair, prepared a Valentine's banquet, ran a pizzeria takeout event, and did roadside cleanup/bottle picking for the municipality. That last event took several days, and on the last day we were all in the back of the pickup ready to head for home when Belinda let out a shriek.

"Stop!"

Her mom, April, who was driving, hit the brakes immediately. Unfortunately, Belinda had already stood up, and the abrupt stop shot her over the side of the pickup. She landed face first in the mud. The thud of her body scared me, and I leaped over the side after her. She didn't move, and I was scared to touch her.

"Belinda?" No answer.

"Belinda!" I heard a shuddering sigh. Finally she slowly rolled over and lifted a hand. I pulled her to a sitting position while she spit mud out and sucked air in. Her mom was out of the driver's seat by then and kneeling with us.

"Are you okay?" She wiped her daughter's face with the edge of her sweater.

Although still wheezing, Belinda managed to nod.

"Why did you scream like that?" I noticed the tremor in April's hand as she dropped the sweater's edge.

"I saw a pop can we missed." At the stunned look on April's face, my laughter erupted. I leaned against the pickup and howled.

Belinda glared at me. "What's so funny?"

"The way you dived off the truck, I thought there was a dead body, or a thousand dollar bill, not a pop can!"

"Hey, that's an extra ten cents for your 'go to Texas' fund."

I tried to control myself. "Yes, and I appreciate it. Now if you could just dive into your geometry like you went after that pop can ..." I dissolved into laughter again as she swatted me.

Our "work-for-you" auction was the biggest fundraiser. We had an evening of snacks and games, and the community could bid on the different students. The bidders then made arrangements for us to come to their place and work for them. Two different people hired me. The first assignment was a day of ironing clothes, visiting, and singing, so I almost felt bad taking the money they gave for such a fun day. But the other bidder had a true job. They were horse ranchers, so I spent the day at their place oiling seventeen saddles, bringing in hay bales, etc. When I was finished, one of the school families dropped in and we all went on a trail ride. I was still very cautious around horses, as an incident in my childhood when my brother was nearly killed by one made me terrified of horses. After a year among these people who lived and worked with horses daily, I'd finally learned to ride Banner, the calmest one in the wranglers' remuda. I had gotten to the place where I almost didn't mind getting on him. Almost. If I had to get on a horse, at least Banner was a great one to have.

With all the different fundraisers, by the time it came to buy our tickets for Texas, we had the money we needed. If there's anything I learned from these people, it was their teamwork. All that hard work for something they weren't going to experience, yet they were so happy to see us go. I was humbled by their generosity.

Chapter 3

Teaching was the reason I had returned to Mayerthorpe, and despite my despair over my brother's death, it was good to have something to keep me occupied. Mind you, at times I almost felt swamped. Math was not my strong suit, and it was the first time I had to teach geometry, so I had to take the course myself. That took many hours after school. While I loved my house, it had only a shower and no laundry facilities, so several people told me to come to their place for baths and laundry. Most of my Saturdays were spent somewhere other than home, and many times people had me come out on Friday evening and stay overnight.

My good friend, Cindy, had me come as much as possible while she still lived there. Her husband was a banker and had been transferred, so they moved a few months after I arrived. An older couple in the church, the Ronalds, had a farm several miles out of town. Daisy was a huge crafter, and I spent many happy evenings at their place learning to make various projects. Lily Aiken, who had been the one to get me into England the previous year, ran a Pioneer's Club, and I helped her with that off and on. Bert's wife, Joyce, ran a concession stand at auction sales and asked me to help occasionally. Sarah Gillis, a school mom, went to farmers' markets, so many Friday evenings I made cinnamon rolls with them and helped set up their booth Saturday morning. The Inksters, another family, invited me over at least once a month. Looking back, I don't know whether these people were just naturally so kind-hearted or if they were making a concerted effort, but I did not lack for things to do that first year while dealing with Nick's death.

Outside of my own personal time, the school and church had many activities to be involved in as well. There were two nursing home services a month that I sang and played for, the youth group had monthly events, and the school had field trips and honour roll trips. When there wasn't a scheduled event happening that winter, often I'd get a phone call.

"Hey, Miss K, we're going over to the Aikens at Blue Ridge. They've got their skating rink cleared. Want to come?"

"What time?"

"Right away. Bring a bag of chips. We're going to do a hot dog roast for supper."

"Sounds good. See you there."

For people who don't grow up in the north, it may seem a lot of work, but we loved to be outside. Skating or sledding in minus twenty-five degrees didn't bother us. We'd build a huge bonfire, and the exercise or standing around the fire with our hotdogs and hot chocolate kept us warm.

For one of the youth activities, Bert rented the public school's gym, which led to an embarrassing moment for me. He and I arrived early to get everything set up for the students. However, twenty seconds after he unlocked the door and we were standing inside, a horrendous shriek started.

I stared at Bert. "What did you do?"

He shrugged. "Nothing."

"Then why is the burglar alarm going? Didn't they know we had rented the place?"

"Yes, but somebody must have forgotten and set the alarm when they left."

My neck muscles bulged as I yelled to be heard above the din. "So turn it off."

"I can't. I don't know the code. Listen, you wait here, and I'll run over to the church and quickly call the police to let them know it's a legal 'break and enter.'"

"Okay, I'll go with you."

"You can't."

"What? Why not?"

"I need you here just in case the police get here before I get back."

I glared at Bert. "Oh great. I'll be deaf *and* get a police record for a 'b and e' because I won't be able to hear what they ask me nor answer correctly, and they'll take me in."

Bert patted my shoulder. "With your imagination, you'll come up with something." He took off at a jog, and I headed over to the office. The door was unlocked, so I went in to see if there was a simple way to stop this noise that was becoming a jack-hammer in my head. When I saw the switchboard with all the plugs, I decided I'd better not mess with anything. Just then a blue and red strobe light started flashing through the office window. I panicked.

Ah Stacy, you bumblehead. If they catch you in the school office, they really won't believe you came in honestly. What were you thinking? Get out of here.

I quickly scooted out and shut the door. Taking a quick look around, I spied a mirrored pillar. An idea popped into my head, and a few minutes later when the police came in through the front door, I was sitting crossed-legged on the floor with all my hair unbraided. My back was to the door and I was singing as I brushed my hair with the brush from my purse. I looked nonchalant, but my nerves were tingling from tension as I waited. Soon two pairs of boots appeared in my peripheral vision. A tap on my shoulder caused me to look up.

"Oh, hello, officers. I apologize for the noise. May I help you?"

"What do you think you're doing?"

"Brushing my hair. I can't braid very well without a mirror." The younger man snorted, while the older guy gave me "the look." Thankfully, before anything else happened, Bert came in with the principal. Within seconds the principal was able to deactivate the alarm, and the piercing vibration through my skull stopped. He apologized.

"I'm so sorry. I forgot to tell the janitor there was a booking here tonight, so he set the alarm before he left."

Bert looked at me. "You never wear your hair down. Why is it like that now?"

The younger policeman grinned. "She was trying to convince us that she broke into the public school to use the mirrored pillar to brush her hair." The men all laughed, but I was not amused.

"Bert! You told me to figure out something. What else was there to do?"

He shook his head. "You could have simply said we were renting the gym, and someone accidently set the alarm on us."

"Oh." They all laughed some more.

I also had a couple incidents with burglar alarms at home. I'd never lived in an alarmed place before, and this dental clinic had two separate alarms. One was for the upstairs offices, and another was for my side door leading down into the basement. I had to get used to setting an alarm whenever I left the basement.

Shortly after I moved in there, one of the school moms needed something I had left at home. I gave her my key to get in and thought nothing of it.

Ten minutes later, I received a phone call from Jill.

"Hello?" A piercing beep sounded.

"Hello? Who's there?"

An annoyed voice responded. "Why didn't you tell me you had an alarm? What's your code?"

"Oops! I'm so sorry; I forgot about it."

"Well, give me the code and then stay on the line. I see police lights. You can explain to the officers why the alarm is going off!"

The second time I had to deal with the dental alarm was harder. It was five o'clock in the morning and suddenly I heard the shrieking of the alarm upstairs. There was no door separating the two floors, so when I heard swearing and banging around, I was sure this time there was a real burglar upstairs.

Ah Stacy! A burglar? What do I do? This dental clinic has been good to me. I can't let somebody rob them of their valuable equipment. But a burglar could be strong. I can't overpower him. Think, Stacy, think!

I grabbed my broom and dustpan and quietly scooted up the stairs. Sitting on the second step, I lodged the broom handle between the stairwell on the first step at ankle height and hoisted the dustpan.

"Excuse me ..." My voice quavered and squeaked, so I cleared my throat and tried again.

"Excuse me, are you a burglar?"

Silence ensued above. I gripped the broom and dustpan tighter.

"Mr. Burglar, could you please come here quickly?"

"I'm not a burglar. I'm the cleaner. What's the confounded code?"

"Oh, well, if you're not a burglar, then the code is ..." I rattled off the number, and a few seconds later, we had blessed relief from the piercing shriek. Shortly thereafter, footsteps headed my way, and soon I was staring at a pair of running shoes. Raising my eyes higher and higher, I eventually reached the face of a woman I'd never seen.

Her frown gradually faded as she looked me over. "Why are you holding a dustpan over your head?"

"Well, if you were a burglar, you were supposed to come running over here, trip over the broomstick, and I'd bonk you on the head as you slid down the stairs."

Puzzlement switched to amusement, and then she started laughing. And laughing. And laughing.

Annoyance overcame my fright. "What's so funny?"

"You. Politely asking if I were a burglar and inviting me over. Thinking a dustpan could do damage. You've read too many Hardy Boy books. You're priceless."

I sheepishly lowered the dustpan. "If you're the cleaning lady, why didn't you know the code?"

"I usually clean in the evenings. The code automatically turns on after I'm done and out of here, so I don't usually need to use it. But I couldn't work last night, so I wanted to get it done before everyone comes this morning."

Flashing police lights showed through the window.

"Oh brother, here I go again."

When I opened the door, Mr. MacLeod, a parent to two of my students, grinned at me. "Miss Kanner, if you really want to get to know all the police in our division, you could just ask me for a tour of our precinct. I'm on desk duty several times a week. There's no need to keep setting off all these alarms." I blushed and he laughed. "I take it there is no problem here, right?"

The cleaning lady laughed and pushed up behind me. "Actually, even if there had been a problem, she had it under control. She was armed and very dangerous. Instead of holding me at gunpoint, she held me 'at dustpan,' and I immediately surrendered." They both laughed while I rolled my eyes. Comedians.

Chapter 4

Having struggled with balance issues most of my life, people often thought I was accident-prone. I'd decided early in life I'd rather be considered the class clown than have people pity me and always want to help me. This year I managed to have an accident at least once a month. I wasn't sure if that was partly from grief clouding my mind, making me less sharp and observant about things as normal. But I sure had people shaking their heads over me many times.

One evening I was at Sarah's house. We were around the wood stove, and I was explaining something. I casually placed a hand square on the stove.

"Y-e-e-o-o-o-w-w!" I hopped madly in anguish while Sarah rushed to the sink and filled a bowl with water. She used one hand to submerge my burned hand in the cool water and placed her other hand against my forehead.

"Are you feeling ok?" Motherly concern oozed out of her.

I jerked my head back. "No, I'm not feeling ok. My hand is killing me."

"So why did you deliberately put your hand on the stove?"

"Because my foot hurt."

Her children burst into howls of laughter. She glared at them, and Molly managed to stop laughing, although her grin split her face. Kent and Faith couldn't stop their giggles.

I sent my own glare toward them. "What is so funny?"

Kent chortled. "What kind of teacher are you? Your foot hurts, so you put your hand on a red-hot stove? Where's the logic in that?"

I managed a shaky grin despite the tears shining in my eyes. "An excellent teacher; I show by example. See, I managed to solve the problem. My hand hurts so badly that I don't feel any pain in my foot right now." The kids burst into laughter again as I continued. "But if you must know, I was simply thinking I'd lean against the wall with my hand and take some of the weight off my foot so it wouldn't hurt so much. The stove just got in the way."

Sarah shook her head and headed for her aloe vera plant.

It was in the same home that I decimated their ping pong table. We'd been having a tournament, and I was in a tight finish with Kent. I'd backed up to manage a spike he'd sent at me, and then he did a light tap to send the ball just over the net. In my forward lunge to try and reach it, I rushed up and tripped on the rug at my feet. I went skidding onto the table, into the net, and the table collapsed with me tangled in the middle. When I managed to extricate myself and sat up, I saw the stunned look on the family's faces and whispered, "Oops." That set off a chain reaction of laughs that brought the dad into the house. He looked at the table, at me, at his wife, and said straight-facedly, "I think we need to increase our insurance for this school year."

I didn't pick on just that family. There were many incidents during youth group and on the school outings that made me a contender for the "Calamity-Jane" title. Flying backwards off the sled going down a hill injured my tailbone. Since I do try to skate but can't stop, a run-in with one student had him getting three stitches in his lip, while I had skate blade slashes on my arm, and gorgeous sunset bruises. I flung myself onto a swing in the park next to a student to chat one day and hadn't noticed the broken steel piece at the edge of it, so I ended up with a two-inch gash along my rib cage. At an overnight slumber party with my girls, we had a pillow fight and I fell off the bed and almost broke my nose on the edge of the desk.

One of my more public embarrassing moments occurred when I was at the West Edmonton mall with the Browns. As we came out of the mall into the wintery, icy snow, somehow I tripped and landed on a shopping cart. It went careening across the parking lot with me half draped over it so I had a lot of bruises from that bar digging into my abdomen before my abrupt halt against a pillar.

Even alone I managed to do damage when I dropped a glass bottle of milk. It shattered and glass was embedded in the top of my feet. It became a school joke that when we went anywhere, we took three emergency First Aid kits along: one for the school and two for me.

Chapter 5

When you're in the dark moments of struggling to cope with grief, it's hard to think of anyone but yourself. In my sorrow and loneliness over losing Nick, I didn't think about what his death meant to my parents. I just knew that although Mom called every so often, Dad never called to talk, so I started to struggle about being adopted once again. One's grief can really mess with the mind. Since Mom would always say Dad was headed to the barn whenever I asked to talk to him, I began to feel I wasn't important to him anymore, and maybe he wished I had died instead of Nick. It never occurred to me that maybe he knew he couldn't talk without crying, or that having another child far away and alone in her grief made him leave the house whenever I called. I knew I was loved, but my insecurity from being adopted tended to easily creep back into my soul.

Finally, three months after I left home, Dad actually called. It was a very awkward conversation, but at least we were able to sort a few things out, and he started joining in on some phone calls after that. It also helped me realize that we all had to deal with our grief in our own way.

Another hard point came at the end of November when I received a package from Cheryl, Nick's wife. Opening it, I found the framed photo of our family picture taken just before Nick died. I was very glad to have it, but looking at it was like having another shaft of glass stabbing and twisting in my wound.

As February drew on, I felt like I was losing my sanity. I was existing on an hour of sleep a night and couldn't figure out what was wrong with me. Suddenly I remembered my Aunt Lucy's talk with me after Nick's funeral.

"I hate to tell you this Stacy—"

"Then don't."

"It might help you down the road."

"What?"

"When a young person dies in an unexpected accident, about six months later, you'll feel worse than you do now."

"That is *so* not what I want to hear."

"But it's true."

"Then just shoot me now and put me out of my misery."

She sighed sadly. "If only it were that easy. This is something only time can help, and it will take a long, long amount of time."

Recalling this conversation one night, I grabbed my calendar and flipped through it.

Wow, Aunt Lucy was right. It's been almost six months and I feel terrible. I sat up in my chair and continued to process my thoughts. *But hey, this is all right. It's normal to feel so abnormal. I'm not going bananas, and I've survived six months of this already. Thanks, God, for having Aunt Lucy tell me this. She knew what she was talking about, having gone through this herself with her son and granddaughter dying in a car accident, too.*

That became a turning point for me. I felt like a bouncy ball emotionally—up and down, up and down. But at least on each bounce downward, my upspring happened quicker and went higher and stayed longer. Just knowing it was okay to feel terrible helped me to acknowledge the grief and keep walking through it one step at a time.

Chapter 6

This isn't to say I was a sad, sobbing mess the whole day long. It was just harder to make myself step out and do things. But I had a lot of fun that year with the school, families, and church people.

Jill approached me the beginning of October.

"We're in charge of our Barrhead church's youth group for this month. We've planned a weekend campout in the Rocky Mountains and were wondering if you'd be willing to come along. We have a speaker but would like your guitar and 'ice-breaker' moments to open each devotions time."

"Sure, sounds like fun. When are you going?"

"Well, most of the teens are taking off school at noon, so we can get down there and set up camp in the daylight. My daughter, Monica, is willing to stay in school all day since you have to teach. Then she'll go with you in your car to help you find us, since we know how easily you get lost." Jill grinned, and I rolled my eyes. She and her husband had to come and find me the first two times I tried to drive to their home in the country.

Arrangements were made and Friday arrived. I had packed my stuff in the car before school, so by 3:30 we were on our way. The few hours' drive to Rocky Mountain House was no problem, but when we turned into the mountains themselves, we hit our first snag.

"Monica, they said to meet us at this river—but this river is twenty-five miles long, and I don't see a sign of them. At which part of the river's length were they going to be waiting?"

"Uh, I actually never asked."

"Oh, great, some navigator you are!"

"Don't panic, Miss K. I'm sure they'll find us."

We actually made a good pair. I was all stressed out for the first two hours, while Monica was calm as a cucumber. Once I realized we had no idea where we were or, more importantly, where they were, I calmed down and planned for a night in the car, while Monica took her turn at being stressed out. I found a small rutted trail up a hill above the road that I pulled my car into so we were out of traffic's way, in case there was any. We ate my snacks and played and sang guitar until it started snowing. Monica's stuff was all with her mom, but thankfully I had mine. We pulled my seats forward in the hatchback area, spread my clothes around for the warmth on the bottom, and used my sleeping bag opened out on top of us to try to stay warm. Monica was able to sleep, but I just rested. The few times I would hear the sound of a vehicle I'd pop into the front seat and blink my headlights. Finally, at 2:30 a.m., the two wranglers searching for us spotted me blinking my lights.

We learned they had been in an unauthorized place, so the entire youth camp had had to move, which was why they weren't even on that river anymore. We had another three-hour drive before we finally pulled into the new camp at 5:30 a.m., just in time to help get breakfast ready for the crowd. Jill greeted me with a grin.

"Even with my daughter, and on a single road, you still can manage to get lost, can't you?"

I laughed. "Hey, everyone has to have some talent. Guess that's mine." I turned to go and help flip pancakes on the big griddle.

It was a great weekend, and a lost night's sleep didn't seem to do anyone any harm.

The next weekend, for Thanksgiving, the Browns invited me to go camping near Jasper with them. They had a small camper on their pickup for themselves and their grandson, Keith, while Belinda and I shared a tent. A few other family and friends joined them either for the day or the weekend. We had a great time, although a storm came through one night.

Something heavy landed across my legs and woke me. I grunted.

"Belinda, get your legs off of me!"

No answer. I shoved at her. "Belinda!"

She growled. "What? Leave me alone."

"Get your legs off of me."

She half sat up but fell back.

"Hey, something's weird—and my legs aren't anywhere near you."

Just then we heard her parents hollering. "Girls, girls, are you all right?"

Belinda responded. "What's going on out there?"

Ethan spoke up. "A tree came down on your tent. Is Stacy also all right?"

I piped in. "I'm fine, but I can't move my legs much."

April laughed shakily. "If you can't move around, then you're not going to be fine for long. I've never known you to stay still before."

"Very funny." I wiggled a bit.

"Don't either of you girls move until we see if we can pull some of these branches away." As the adults started to scrape and tug at things, we could hear Keith's plaintive voice. "How cool! It's not fair. Why do the girls get to have all the fun, while I have to sleep in the camper with you?"

By now a few of their friends in the next campsite had awakened, and with their extra help it wasn't too long before Belinda and I were able to crawl through the tent opening. We turned and looked at the smashed-in tent. Belinda turned to me. "Don't you know students are supposed to get in trouble *from* their teachers, not *because* of their teachers?"

My mouth dropped. "Because? How on earth is our crushed tent supposed to be my fault?"

She shrugged as she grinned. "Things always happen to you, not me. So therefore, it must be because of you!"

April gave us both a thorough inspection, but we hadn't been hurt at all. "Your guardian angels must have had a busy night! I can't believe that tree landed all around you and never hurt you!"

As I looked at that tree, my mind flashed back a month to the tree landing on the camper van Cheryl and I had been in. *Lord, are you trying to get my attention about something? Two trees in two months land on me, yet I'm unscathed. Believe me, I'm listening.*

When you feel like you want to give up on life during your dark days of grief, remember the escape from falling trees and how good it felt to be alive immediately afterward.

Good point, Lord. I am thankful to be alive, even when I don't feel it.

You are loved, and you are not walking through this valley alone. Now you will be able to empathize and help others when they struggle through their valleys.

During the days of camping with the Browns, we took several hikes. Ethan chose the first one.

"If you have the stamina, we can pack a lunch and head for this mountain peak. It's a beautiful view from the top of a waterfall."

Of course, the challenge that we might not have what it took to get up there was all it took to get us started on the trail. Hours later I was wondering where my brain had gone as we hiked over rocks and boulders on this imaginary trail we were supposedly following. Ethan kept encouraging us.

"We've gone too far to turn back now … we're over halfway. We can't stop now … that's not really a boulder, just an oversized rock." Finally we slid off the last boulder and found—

"Shale! I give up." I slumped back against the boulder and rested my aching calves.

"Shale means we're nearly at the top." Mr. Brown grinned at me and tossed down a water bottle. "Keith's going to make it; don't tell me you can't outdo a six-year-old." I gritted my teeth and started the long two-steps-forward, slide-back-one shuffle to get to the peak.

When we reached the summit and walked across to the falls—oh my! Although we hadn't climbed clear to heaven, "next-door-to-Paradise" stretched out before us. I sighed in utter contentment and slid my eyes over to Ethan. He tipped his head at me and smiled. It had been worth the climb.

Thankfully, going down was a lot easier, but my calves were screaming at me when I limped into camp and sank onto a log by the fire.

Ethan gave me a ribbing. "What's wrong with you? It was only ten kilometres. Teaching must be making you soft."

I didn't even open my eyes as I answered. "Ten kilometres of that kind of stuff is at least twenty kilometres of normal walking."

April joined us around the fire. "Well, don't worry; Ethan, you had your fun today. Tomorrow I pick the hike, and it's going to be a real trail."

She was true to her word and picked a lovely forested trail that didn't have us bounding over boulders. The only problem was that she picked one that seemed to go straight up, and it was twelve kilometres long instead of ten. My legs were quivering by the time we returned. I was extremely grateful that on Monday we had a leisurely special brunch and then packed up. We hiked only Malone Canyon on our way out, and compared to the other two, that one was a breeze. It was a Thanksgiving to remember—and the day after we returned home, it snowed.

Some other memorable events were done with the school. This school always had great honour roll trips, so every effort was made by the students to earn the right to go on them. For the fall trip we took them to the Canadian Finals rodeo in Edmonton, the second was a ski trip to Rabbit Hill (close to Edmonton), and the third was usually camping. This was a very outdoorsy group, and it was a pleasure to spend time with the students outside of the classroom doing fun things.

Chapter 7

Right after Thanksgiving (in October in Canada), my dad's oldest sister, Aunt Ruby, called me.

"Stacy, I can't get you off my mind. You lost your brother, and you're all alone out in Alberta."

"I'm okay, Aunt Ruby. I have good days and bad days, but the people here are very good to me."

"But they aren't family. So I was wondering …"

"Yes?"

"I'm planning to go to Florida for a couple of months. Would you like to come and spend Christmas with me there?"

I was flabbergasted. "Wow! I don't know. Uhmmm … I'll have to think about it, but thanks!"

That occupied my mind for the next few days. When I learned how much a plane ticket would cost, I didn't think I could do it, but the thought of a warm Florida during the coldest, darkest days of Alberta just wouldn't leave. Then my brother Jason called. He and his wife, Rose, were working on Christmas plans themselves.

"Stacy, how are you doing?"

"Living, I guess."

"That doesn't sound great."

"Well, it's dark and cold, and that doesn't help one's mental state."

"I understand that. As a matter of fact, Rose and I have been talking about going to Florida for Christmas. Her brother has just moved down there, so we'd like to go and see their new place. It will give us a chance to get away from our Illinois winter, too."

I screeched into the phone. "W-h-a-a-t?"

Jason's voice sounded puzzled. "What's 'what?'"

"Oh, sorry. It's just so weird that you and your wife want to go to Florida. Aunt Ruby has just invited me to spend Christmas with her—in Sarasota, where Grandpa and Grandma Kanner had their cottage."

Jason chuckled. "God moves in mysterious ways; that's not far from where we'll be. It would be so nice to spend some brother/sister time. Why don't we see about getting you a ticket to Florida, and then you can drive back with us to Illinois and fly back to Alberta from there."

I hung up the phone and looked at the ceiling.

Thanks, God. I didn't realize how much I was missing my family. I can live on bread and water for the next six weeks if you can just make this work so I can get away.

You're welcome, my child. In the midst of pain and suffering, there is always the chance for joy when you choose to look for it.

I scraped my pennies together, and not only did I manage to cover the cost of the plane tickets, but for Christmas, instead of giving me gifts, the school and church donated money and gave me a cheque that enabled me to have some spending money as well.

Unfortunately, the start of this much-needed vacation didn't go so well. Three days before I was to leave, I came down with strep throat, tonsillitis, and the flu all at the same time. I was so miserable on the way to the plane that I wasn't sure I wanted to go. It was an excruciating flight for me, as my ears wouldn't adjust to the air pressure, and for the first three days in Florida, everyone sounded as if they were underwater. But both the warm weather and the oranges I could pick off the tree to eat managed to cure me. Soon I enjoyed hunting for shark teeth along the beach with my aunt, helping her quilt group with the quilt they were making, seeing my first alligator, and spending an evening on a boat tour. Three dolphins decided we were their play toy, and they followed in the wake of our boat almost half an hour, leaping in arcs into the air as a trio. I called them Faith, Hope, and Charity. Such a random, spectacular time with those dolphins gave me a peace and renewal of spirit as we returned to shore.

My brother and his family picked me up on December 29, and we made it back to Arthur, Illinois, just in time for me to join the youth group for the New Year's Eve party. It'd been five years since I'd taught there, so it was good to catch up with everyone, although I was a bit nostalgic as I looked around and realized how many things had changed. It made me realize I needed to savour every moment I'd been given, because as I knew all too well with Nick, nothing lasts forever.

Chapter 8

By the end of January, I'd received a couple of job offers to various schools. I asked the Alberta school if they wanted me to stay on for another year, and they said they'd discuss it at the next board meeting. While waiting for that, I received a letter from Peru that intrigued me. A chance to go overseas again tugged at me. The letter was hard to understand, as the English wasn't the greatest. This was the very reason they wanted an English person to come to their school— to help them learn English properly.

I always ran my options for work past my parents. I valued their input. So far, they had always been very supportive of everywhere I was asked to go. But when I talked to Dad about this place, he was hesitant.

"Have you prayed about this, Stacy?"

"Well, I just got the letter, so not much yet. Why?"

"I don't know—there's a lot there that concerns me."

"Like what?"

"You said the letter wasn't written well. That's a Spanish country, so will you have people there that can communicate with you in English?"

"I don't know—this guy, Javi, is writing on behalf of his father, who is the pastor of the church. They have over one hundred students and want to use the ACE (Accelerated Christian Education) books, which are mostly in English, so they need help learning a second language. Javi has taken a few years of English at the Lima university."

"It sounds like this could be a very tough position."

"Why?"

"Stacy, you're still grieving your brother's death. To leave Canada to go into a country where you know no one and can't speak their language—it's your choice, of course, but you need to seriously pray about this one. Has the school in Alberta asked you to come back?"

"Not yet, but they're going to talk about it at the next board meeting."

"If they want you back, then maybe the best thing would be to accept that."

"What about Peru?"

"They're in the opposite hemisphere, so they probably have school when you don't. My suggestion would be to offer to go to Peru for the summer. That way you'd have only a few months down there, yet it would give you a chance to see how that school is run. If you like it, you can return to teach in Alberta for the year while making plans to head back to Peru for a full year following that."

After praying, sending letters back and forth to Peru, and receiving a request to teach another year in Mayerthorpe, that's what I decided to do. To my surprise, April Brown came to me one day.

"Stacy, Ethan and I have been talking."

I cocked an eyebrow. "That's good to know. Since you're married, I'd hope you'd do that frequently." I smirked as she mock-glared at me.

"We were wondering if you'd consider taking Belinda to Peru with you?"

Since her comment came out of left-field, it blindsided me. "What?"

"Belinda is graduating this spring. She's not sure yet what she wants to do with her life. We think a chance to go overseas would be an eye-opener for her."

"April, I have no idea what I'm getting into down there."

"We know. That's why, since you and Belinda get along so well, we thought it might be good to have a familiar face along with you."

I hummed a bit. April saw the look on my face. "What is it?"

I looked around their house. "April, you have such a beautiful place here. I have the feeling from the few things I can figure out through these letters that I might be going into somewhat of a 'third-world-country' area. Belinda is used to nice things."

"That's another reason we'd like her to go with you. It would do her good to see how other people have to live." She patted my arm. "Just pray about it. We'll be okay with whatever decision you make."

I really stewed over that request. Because I was headed into the unknown, I was extremely hesitant to take someone with me. What if something bad happened? I called my parents once again.

"Mom, Dad, the Browns want me to take their daughter with me to Peru. I don't know what to say."

"Why are you hesitant about it?" Mom's voice sounded serene.

"Because Belinda is from a well-to-do family compared to where I think I might be going to stay."

Dad's voice came over the line. "Do you get along with her well?"

"Of course—well, except when it's time to do math. She has more excuses than a dictionary has words about that subject!"

Mom entered the conversation again. "Did the Browns ask you, or did you ask them?"

"They asked me." Mom chuckled. "What's so funny?"

"It's amazing how God answers prayer. Your dad and I have a real hesitancy about this trip, and we were talking about how nice it'd be if you weren't going alone. Now God has offered a travelling companion. We think that is a good thing. Keep praying about it."

"Okay. I will."

Belinda herself was the one who finally made my decision for me. She barged into my room one evening.

"Look, I know my parents have asked you to let me go to Peru with you. But you haven't said yes or no. What's the problem? Do you not want me to go? Just say so, then."

"Belinda, it's not that I don't like you."

"Then what is it?"

"You have such a nice place, and I'm scared that where I'm going, it might be pretty rugged."

Belinda rolled her eyes. "For Pete's sake, you know what our weeklong camping trips are like. Do you see me whining and complaining about the dirt on those?"

I stared at her in surprise. She did have a point. "True, but that's only a week; this will be almost three months."

"If you can hack it, I can."

"Do you really want to go?"

"If you want me, yes."

I grinned at her. "All right then. My parents and your parents both think this is a good idea, so let's do it."

She laughed. "But let me graduate first, okay?"

So plans were made for graduation to be June 20. We also wanted to go on the annual camping trip into the Rockies, so we bought tickets to leave right after Canada Day (July 1).

In the meantime, there were plenty of things to occupy my time. The beginning of March I started having car trouble. Friends who did most of their own mechanical work offered to work on my car so I took it out to them. First it was the clutch, then the crankshaft, and on and on. It was the end of April before they had it fixed, and my pocketbook was rather empty. It was a good thing I'd bought the Peruvian plane ticket before the car broke down.

Molly and I finished memorizing the book of Proverbs for convention. The school families pitched in to do enough fundraisers so we could fly to Texas, where the International Student Convention was being held. Memorizing a book of the Bible received an automatic first place ribbon there. These church people felt that such memory work was worth their efforts to raise the money for a student to attend ISC.

I was able to catch a ride with one of the families from school to Vanderhoof, British Columbia, to spend my spring break with the Burtons. Even though I spent only one year with them in Oregon and I didn't see them often, they had told me I was part of their family. This year it was extra-special to be at their place. Jean was getting married the beginning of May, so Noreen, Amy, Mattie, and I were involved in helping her. My brothers had married away from our home, so we just showed up for their weddings. This was my first experience helping a bride—and what a busy week it was. Taste-testing food for the wedding, picking out the flowers, colours, and a huge array of fun things had to be done. We still found time to gather around the musical instruments, and Jean and I played some tennis.

"Jean, you've eaten too many different foods tasting stuff for the wedding. You're slowing down." I grinned at her as I won a game and we hung puffing at the net.

She tossed her racquet at me. "I just figured you're getting old and I'd better go easy on you." Then she paused. "But I would like to give you my racquet, to remember me by."

I gaped at her. "Why? You're getting married, not buried!"

She laughed. "Only you would say something like that."

"But why give me your racquet? You'll still play after you're married."

"You've been such a friend to me. I never knew a teacher could actually be a friend as well as a teacher until you came along." I blinked my eyes rapidly. "Sorry, I didn't mean to make you cry."

My hand swiped at my eyes. "Not crying. Wind's picking up."

She laughed. "Well, I have a favour to ask of you."

"What?"

"After the reception, we're having an open mic, but also a few planned things. I'd like you to write a song and sing it for us."

I stared at her. "I write poetry, not songs."

"You can use an old familiar tune and just put words to it for us. Please?"

"Well, after you gave me such a compliment, I can't really say, no, now can I?"

"Great!"

Right after spring break, my school arrived in Vanderhoof for the three-day ACE convention. We had a great time and won a few awards. I returned to Mayerthorpe on a beautiful spring morning with the students in the big old fifteen-passenger van Sarah let us borrow. Bert was driving and I was in the front passenger seat when Belinda piped up.

"Steven isn't feeling well. The rolling hills of the Rockies are getting to his stomach."

I pulled out the ice cream bucket and the 7-Up we always carried for such occasions. He sipped away at it, and we rolled the windows down. Soon he thrust the can up beside me.

"Thanks, Miss K. I do feel better, but I don't want to drink all this."

"Okay. That's fine." I took the can from him but didn't want to put it in the garbage with liquid still in it. So I simply thrust my hand out the window, turned the can upside down, and let the liquid flow out.

"Aaayyy-ooowwww!" Shrieks from the back of the vehicle caused Bert to swerve the van, and the can dropped out of my hand. I whipped around and looked at the kids. Steven was covered with a fine sheen.

"What happened to you?" I puzzled at the glare some kids were giving me.

Steven wiped his face and rolled his eyes. "Miss K, both windows are open. When you dumped the pop, the force of the wind blew it all in through our window!"

My eyebrows shot up. I bit my lip. "Oops." The kids that hadn't received any of the sticky substance hooted with laughter. "Well, you made me litter. You scared me so badly with that yell, I dropped the can on the highway. Guess we're even."

Steven sighed. "That's not as bad as getting drenched with sticky stuff, and you know it."

At our next stop, we had to pull out the suitcases to get him a clean shirt.

The end of April was tough for a couple reasons. The dentist informed me that the Public Health Unit was going to rent the basement, so I would have until the end of May to move out. That gave me a month to find a place to store my belongings and decide what to do. When my sister-in-law found out I was going to be homeless, she sent me a large surprise package.

I came home from work and found it at my doorstep. I opened the note.

Never say that you don't have a home anymore.

Puzzled, I tore open the package. To my surprise, I found a lovely two-man tent. She sent that to me as a joke, but for these past thirty years, I've used that many times on my travels. It was one of the best practical jokes she ever gave me.

The other struggle involved my health. Mrs. Brown contacted the Health Unit and found out there were several shots we needed to take to go to Peru. Normally a person was to take the necessary shots once a month over the course of half a year. Now we had to get yellow fever, cholera, hepatitis, malaria, and a few other shots all within six weeks. Belinda seemed to have no problem with them, but I've always been quite sensitive to medication, and getting so much so quickly did an awful number on me. I was so sick for a few weeks that I wasn't sure the disease would have been much worse.

At least I was well enough to drive back through the Rockies the beginning of May to attend Jean's wedding. It was a beautiful event, and I feel my poem/song went well. But the crowning moment of the event for me was when she went to throw her bouquet. A large crowd had gathered round, with me way at the back. I hated that kind of stuff, but I knew she wanted me to get the bouquet so was going to heave it in my direction. She was up a set of steps and her husband twirled her so her back was to us. I don't know if she got dizzy or nervous, but instead of throwing behind her to the girls below, she threw upwards and sideways. The next thing we knew, her bouquet had landed in the candelabra, which still had candles burning in it. As soon as I realized her flowers were starting to smoke, I started laughing. One of the men, with great presence of mind, leapt forward, yanked them out of the candles, and stomped on them. He held the squashed bouquet up and sheepishly tried to hand them to the girl next to him. I tried to stop laughing as one of the other girls glared at me.

"What's so funny about this? Those poor flowers. I intended to catch them."

I choked down a giggle. "I taught her well."

"What do you mean?"

"I've always said, 'Don't follow the crowd; be yourself.' Just think—anyone can throw a bouquet of flowers. But to add a touch of the flame thrower to that tradition … now that's memorable!" I could see the young lady didn't appreciate my sense of humour, so I excused myself to go and laugh in private.

Chapter 9

It took a bit of scrambling for me to dismantle my home. Between going to Jean's wedding, packing to take Molly to Texas for ISC, packing for a summer down in Peru, packing to put everything in storage, and packing for what I needed to survive a month living on the run, May was a crazy month. One of the families on a farm offered a shed for me to use, so several people with trucks came and helped. On May 20, I walked out of my home for the last time. I admit I did some sniffling; it had been a good home for me. Many of the families offered their homes, so I spent a few days here and a few days there and only used my car/tent for a few nights during my few homeless months.

On May 23 Molly and I flew to Texas. At our second boarding gate, we ran into a few other Albertans headed to the same spot, and they offered us a lift on the bus they had rented, so that was a blessing.

The week in Texas flew by. Molly and I both suffered from sunburn, as we weren't used to such intense heat. We watched various performances, met interesting people, and were invited to go shopping with some of them. Naturally, being from cowboy country, we came home with a pair of cowboy boots for Molly and a Stetson for me. After the first sunburn, I just wanted something to cover my poor neck, and that was the most logical thing to find in Texas.

Molly had entered a quilt in the sewing section. When we toured the art and craft buildings, we saw there were twenty-four quilts entered, so Friday morning when she was called to the podium, we were ecstatic to find she had placed second.

Once back, I had the end of the school year to finish up. Belinda and Steven were both graduating, so the push was on to finish their last books. Of course, in spring students aren't as willing to buckle down and work, so we had a bit of stress, as their last tests were the day before graduation. But they both passed, and graduation was a great day.

We had two weeks to enjoy the youth group outings, the Rocky Mountain campout, and the buying of supplies that we thought might be important for a three-month stay in Peru. Cramming it all in our suitcases was another major undertaking. We enjoyed Canada Day holiday with everyone, checked our passports, our money, and our nervous systems. Then finally, on July 3, we got up at 4:00 a.m. for Belinda's parents to drive us into Edmonton to the airport. As we waved a tearful goodbye to them, we had no idea the events that would change and shape us over the next ten weeks. We were just a nineteen and a twenty-four-year-old out to have an adventure and help some people.

Chapter 10

I had travelled overseas twice by now, so felt I'd be good with this trip. Edmonton to Calgary to Salt Lake City to Los Angeles was not a problem. However, the L.A. airport was huge and we had to change airlines there, which I hadn't done before.

Belinda moved closer to me. "Wow, there's a lot of people here."

"Uh-huh."

"I've never heard so many different languages all at one time."

"Uh-huh."

"You don't have a clue what you're doing, do you?"

"Nuh-huh. But not to worry; there's no way I can lose you with that huge pillow you're lugging around!"

Belinda's elbow gave a quick jab into my side. "Never you mind about my pillow."

Her pillow had been a bone of contention for the past two weeks. She'd asked me if she should take it. Because it was a huge, down-stuffed, oversized monstrosity, I said it would be a pain. She waffled back and forth about it and decided to leave it at home. As we got in the car that morning to leave, she suddenly turned around, dashed inside, and returned with a mutinous expression on her face. "Don't say it; I'll take care of it, but it is going. I need something familiar down there, and I love my pillow."

So it came—and it was a pain. Because the L.A. airport was filthy, she didn't want it to touch the ground, and we resorted to many different measures to keep it above knee level. At least it was light, although bulky.

By continually asking people, we managed to bumble our way to the proper gate within the allotted hours and made our final lap to Lima. Already I was thankful to have Belinda along; my anxiety at what lay ahead was mitigated by having someone else to share the adventure.

Peruvian customs were a bit of a nightmare, as I only knew about five words of Spanish. This is when the reality of what we were doing sank in. As we stood in line, a woman approached.

"Ustedes touristas?"

I slowly nodded.

"Pasaportas."

Belinda and I looked at each other. I shrugged and gave her our passports. She glanced at them. "Vamos."

From her waving hand, we moved to another man. He pointed to an aisle. "Vamos."

As we moved that way, another man started waving at us and yelling. We didn't get that, but his hand motions told us to stop. The first man continued to wave us on, while the second man insisted we stop. The first man thrust our passports into our hands and faced off with the other man. While they were having an increasingly vocal dispute, a third man appeared, looked at both of us, and whispered, "Vamos, vamos."

Bel looked at me, and I looked at her. I shrugged. "Guess we've learned our first word here, so let's 'vamos.'" She laughed and we left. When we felt it safe to stop, I looked at my passport. "That's weird."

"What is?"

"They never stamped our passports."

"Is that bad?"

"Well, I hope we don't have trouble getting out of the country. I think we're supposed to have a stamp in here. At least my other two countries always stamped them. Oh well, I'm not going back to see. They seemed awfully upset about something back there."

As we exited the immigration area and stood looking around for who might be Javi, we had no idea that we had just arrived in the midst of a terrorist uprising. Sendero Luminoso, the Shining Path guerrillas, had just taken over the city. We just knew it was 1:00 a.m. and we'd been up since 4:00 a.m. the previous morning. I was tired, scared, and wondering why on earth we'd come.

As I blinked, wearily scanning the airport, a young man approached.

"I'm Javi. You must be Estaci."

My legs almost buckled with relief. "Yes, I'm Stacy, and this is Belinda."

He shook our hands and led us over to his father, who greeted us warmly in Spanish. Javi slowly started to translate, and I soon understood why they wanted native English speakers. He had a grasp of basic English, but it was very hard to understand him, and he had to think a lot to be able to tell us what his father said.

"Welcome. We are so surprised and glad to see you here."

I shot a puzzled look at Belinda and slowly replied. "Surprised? We said we'd come and gave you the dates. Do you mean 'happy?'"

He shook his head. "We didn't think you'd show up. We came to the airport just in case."

Now my knees really buckled. I sank to the nearest chair. "Well, now I'm surprised, but so glad you did the 'just in case,' or I wouldn't have an idea what to do next. Why didn't you think we'd come?"

"Most people don't do what they say."

Belinda frowned. "Well, we *do* do what we say we will."

The dad spoke to Javi and walked away. Javi settled down into a chair.

Again Bel and I exchanged puzzled glances. "Javi, why did your dad leave, and why are you sitting here? We have our luggage, so we're good to go with him." I was a bit snippy from lack of sleep.

Javi shrugged. "We can't leave until 6:00, so Dad went to get us some drinks."

My eyebrows shot up. "It's only 1:30 right now. Why on earth are we not leaving until 6:00?"

Javi shrugged once more. It was something I would have to learn to deal with during those ten weeks—the ability to shrug off things that I couldn't change. "The guerillas have imposed a curfew; no one is allowed out from 10:00 p.m. to 6:00 a.m.

Two things hit me, and I didn't know which to address first. "Guerrillas? You've been here since 10:00 waiting for us?"

Javi's face turned bleak and forlorn. "My country—it is in trouble. Sendero Luminoso is muy poderoso." (As our time went by, Javi became quite proficient in English. I gave him a private lesson every day. He was a quick learner and had an aptitude for language, but at the beginning we both had a struggle. I had to learn to speak very slowly, and he had to think and switch out the Spanish words for the English ones.) "Path of the Shining Light. Very powerful. And no, not ten o'clock. Eight o'clock. We had to come in on the bus that had to be back to our city by 10:00 p.m."

"How long of a bus ride is it?"

"About two hours."

I groaned. I hadn't been in the country more than an hour and already I realized I would have to learn patience.

Lord, why did you bring me here? I can't stand waiting around.

My child, that is precisely why this will be good for you. Patience is something you struggle with.

Exactly. So can't I just fail this test and get on with the next one?

This will help you become a better person.

I thought you loved me just the way I am?

I do.

Soooo?

And too much to let you stay just that way.

Aaah, this will be so hard.

I'll be here with you.

Belinda was a night owl, so it wasn't as hard for her to sit and wait out the next four hours. By the time we boarded the bus, my eyes were scratchy from lack of sleep. However, we were only on the road a short time before my adrenaline kicked in and I was wide awake.

The road we were on was narrow and winding, and we were on the outside ledge of a mountain. Far below I could see the ocean, which was fine. What was petrifying was the crumpled remains of various vehicles dotted here and there among the rocks and boulders. A couple of times as we swerved around a curve, I looked out and couldn't see any road below me. Bel leaned over once, took a look, and promptly shut her eyes.

"Boy, am I glad you took the window seat!"

I looked over at Javi. He was peacefully eating a banana.

"Javi, there are a lot of pieces of metal and buses down there."

"Si, many bad accidents along here. So bad they shut down the bus lines for a while."

"How long have they been running again?"

"A couple weeks."

My back jerked forward on the seat. "Only a couple weeks? How do they know it's safe to go again?"

Javi flipped the banana peel out the window and shrugged. "All bad bus drivers dead." He closed his eyes.

I slumped back in my seat while Bel giggled. "Guess that solves the problem in his mind."

When we arrived at their home, to my dismay, we weren't allowed to go to bed. We had to be introduced to his mother, his two younger brothers, Diego and Jovany, and the little sister, Sofia. Then Javi insisted on taking us on a tour of their place. I was almost punch drunk from lack of sleep and was getting increasingly angry that they wouldn't let us go to bed. I stumbled around after him but couldn't focus or concentrate. What I didn't realize until later was they didn't have a bed for us. They didn't believe we would actually come, so Javi had to divert us while they prepared a place for us.

The two younger boys gave up their beds and either squeezed in with Javi in his bed or slept on the concrete floor so that we could have their narrow, slat-board cots. They hauled them up to the second floor over the church (which was attached to their house via a courtyard) and put the two cots there. Then the dad returned to town to purchase two blankets for us to use.

Thirty-three hours after leaving Alberta, we were finally left in a small concrete room with bars on the window and a light bulb dangling a foot from the ceiling by its electrical cord. This was the church's small office, but they cleared it out so we could have a bedroom. We looked at each other in our grimy, weary, and exhausted state.

"Home, sweet home," I mumbled as I flopped onto the nearest cot.

Bel managed a shaky grin. "At least I have a pillow." She hit the other cot, and that's the last either of us said for a good many hours.

Chapter 11

Once we had some good sleep under our belts, we felt we could function again. Javi's family was so good and gracious to us, but the culture shock was intense. We were both small town, country-style girls, and now we were in the middle of a city of 80,000 people. A very poor city by the looks of it.

"Stacy, it looks like we're in a war zone," Bel stared out our barred windows at a bleak, barren landscape. "There's one lone tree down below us, and that's the only green I see."

Although Javi had shown us everything the day before, neither of us could remember anything, so we went exploring again. Next to our room was the communal bathroom. It was a full-sized room, which surprised us. We didn't realize at the time that it was the only bathroom for the two hundred plus people that attended church here. There was a concrete trench with a couple of taps, and a broken mirror above it. One entire side wall was a long urinal, while on the opposite side of the room were two stalls. They had toilets in them but no cover on one tank, and no seat on the other.

Bel tried both taps. "Stacy, there's only cold water."

"Maybe it takes a while for the hot to make it up here."

We went into the hall and poked our noses into a couple of rooms. We assumed they were the classrooms, as there were a couple of tables and a blackboard. As we continued downstairs, Bel put her hand through the window. "There's no glass in the windows here."

"Well, at least our room has glass, although I'm not sure why they have bars."

We crossed the auditorium of the church and opened the door. We entered into the enclosed courtyard. There was a type of cistern built against the far wall, and close to it a small shower. We peered in and Bel yelped.

"What's wrong?"

"Don't you see?"

"See what?"

"Look!" Bel pushed my face toward the back wall. "There's only one tap. That means they don't have hot water."

"Ooh. Yeah. Right."

From our upper bedroom window, we had noticed that part of their house roof was thatch, part just a slab of concrete, and one area a corrugated section of tin lay over the open area. When we walked in there, we saw one small sink with a tap in the kitchen and a little two-burner gas stove. The mom had an old-fashioned wringer-washer that could be used when the power was on. We soon learned that was maybe 40% of the time.

Although we were appalled at the poverty we saw, or thought we saw, when Javi's mom, Elena, took us with her Sunday afternoon for a Bible study in a nearby neighbourhood, we realized we were living with a well-to-do family. Many of these people had houses made of sticks leaning together with cloth draped over. The floors were dirt, and the children had no shoes. But they were still gracious and offered us their best.

When we got back home, Bel turned to me.

"Welcome to the castle."

I grinned. "Yeah, there's nothing like real poverty to make one realize how much one has. Yesterday I was shocked that Elena had only six china plates. But after what we saw today, this is high class. We have a table and good plates for most of us. We can also go into their living room and sit on a couch or a chair—and they even have a footstool to put my feet up on."

Having said that, I moved to the chair, plopped my feet on the beautiful faux leather stool in front of me, and relaxed. To my astonishment, my legs shifted a bit to the left.

"W-h-a-a-t?" I moved my legs in front of me and watched. They soon slid sideways. Then I gaped as an ugly neck craned out and around. I stared in horror as a pair of lidless, cobalt, rocky eyes glared at me.

At that moment, Sofia burst into the room, blabbing away. I couldn't understand a word she said and was frozen in shock at the evil eyes staring me down. Sofia left the room and soon returned, dragging Javi with her.

He smiled and smoothed her hair. "Sofia wants to know why you're kicking her pet."

That broke through my zombie-mode. I jumped up. "Pet? I thought it was a footstool."

From my different perspective, I could now see the massive tortoise was indeed alive and not a piece of the furniture. Sofia held out a bamboo stick that was bigger than two of my fingers. The tortoise snapped it in two and chewed on a piece while still balefully glaring at me. I gulped while Belinda snorted with laughter.

"Way to make a friend, Stacy!"

"How was I to know it wasn't furniture? It didn't move, and it's just the size and shape of a fancy footstool."

"Well, he doesn't look like he's gonna forget you any time soon."

I looked at Javi. "Is he dangerous?"

Javi shrugged. "He's a snapping turtle so has powerful jaws. But Sofia rescued him as a baby, and I think he truly is fond of her. He'll let her ride on his shell, but he's not close with anyone else here."

I shuddered. "Close! Sheesh." I promptly named him Dracula, and he and I kept wary eyes on each other the rest of the time I lived there.

The day after we arrived, we had to change our money. Again, a different culture made it much more difficult for us and dependent on Javi. Javi was a few years younger than I was, and I felt bad he was burdened with the sole care of these two strange girls, but we couldn't have survived without him.

We followed him when he said come, but instead of going into a bank, he just stopped by a man on the street and talked. Then he motioned for us to pull out our money. Soon we were surrounded and pressed in by a crowd of men. Belinda had one man fingering the edge of her purse, while another was touching me. I yelled.

"Javi!" He looked over and said something. The men backed off briefly, but not much. I have claustrophobia and couldn't get away soon enough.

When we managed to break free, Javi explained something. "I'm sorry about that, but haven't you noticed everyone following you and touching you?"

"Yes, but those were kids yesterday. These are grown men."

"You have to understand how unique you are. I've been to the capital to university, so I've seen a few white people occasionally. Here, no one has seen a white person before. It's like your people going to the zoo to look at the monkeys." He grinned when I huffed. "You'll have to get used to it more than Belinda. At least she has brown hair and brown eyes and a darker complexion. But you—blonde hair, blue eyes, and such fair skin; people here are very superstitious. They're half terrified, half in awe of you."

He was right. The entire time I was in Peru, I had people from children to the elderly whisper about me, touch me, pinch me, and try to scratch my eyes to see if the blue would come off. It was quite disconcerting. Since I bruise easily, after the first few pinches I had purple, green, blue, and yellow discolouration on my arms. My bruises convinced them I was magical, so I was constantly getting pinched to see what colour my white skin would change into. I couldn't get them to understand what bruises were, since their skin never turned such colours as mine did.

Because the constant touching and pinching were becoming a problem, we figured out a solution. Belinda had borrowed a friend's high-quality camera, and I had my ordinary one along, so we made an agreement that we'd use hers to take photos and then just have doubles made. That way I left my film out of my camera and used it to fend off people. Because of their superstitions, many street people were terrified of the flash on the camera going off. They thought it was the devil come to grab their souls. If my flash went, they would flee away from us. I felt terrible about using that fear to make life easier for me, but I didn't know how else to stop being used like a pin cushion.

Our big concern was letting our parents know we were alive and in Peru. Unfortunately, a telephone was a luxury few could afford. There was a public telephone exchange building several blocks from Javi's home. When we got there, we could put our request in to an operator. Then we sat in the rows of chairs waiting until our name was spoken over the intercom, telling us that the connection had been made. We waited up to an hour several times the first week there, but the connection between Lima and Canada was down. We quickly learned the term "otra vez" (try again) when wanting to call home.

Meanwhile, back in Canada, the Browns had learned that all Canadians had been evacuated from Peru due to the "explosive situation." Mrs. Brown called Ottawa to let them know that two Canadian girls were still in-country.

"I'm sorry, Ma'am. The Canadians have all been pulled out of the country.

It's too dangerous for foreigners to be there at the moment."

"Well, there are two girls down there right now. I know. One is my daughter."

"Again, Ma'am, the Canadians are gone. We've checked the embassy list and contacted all personnel."

"They probably didn't register at the embassy. They just arrived in the country."

"Tell them to contact us within the next few days or they won't be able to get out at all. We're closing the embassy until the war between the present government and the guerrillas subsides."

"I can't contact them. There's no phone where they are. I have to wait until they can find a way to call."

"I'm sorry; there's nothing we can do."

The call ended and left April Brown with nothing to do but pray fervently that we'd make contact. When Belinda finally got a connection to her parents and we heard this, we still had to convince Javi's dad to take us to the embassy. His philosophy was, "If God wants you to be dead, you'll be dead." That was all well and good, but we were angry that he unilaterally made that decision for us. A week later, he finally agreed to take us to the capital. Although the Canadian Embassy was closed, I'd come into Peru on an American passport, so I felt we'd both be accepted there.

We came around the corner of the street on which the American embassy was located. As I looked at the pile of rubble of the bombed building strewn along the street and saw soldiers running ruthlessly about, the gravity of our situation hit me hard.

God, why did you bring us down here if we're just going to die?

I am here in the good and the bad.

Well, this is definitely the bad! I don't understand. We could have just stayed in Canada.

You will learn about Me here in ways you've never known.

Javi's dad quickly pulled us into a side street. We kept our faces down while Javi and his dad blocked us from the soldiers' views. We made our way back to the bus stop and were able to catch the next one back to our city. Belinda and I didn't speak the entire trip home.

In retrospect, I am amazed and humbled at the fortitude of this family in keeping these two foreigners alive and safe. It must have been a huge strain on them. I'm sure I wasn't always the most respectful of their ways when I fluctuated between fear and anger that I couldn't understand what was going on and why. But one thing I learned quickly was that when they said to come or go, I simply did it. You don't stop to ask why when your life is on the line.

Chapter 12

We had a couple of days to settle in before school started. Besides their paper business in the front of their house, this family had a small farm half-an-hour drive outside the city. The dad had a small dirt bike on which he took his family. Jovany balanced on the handles, while Elena sat sideways on the seat behind her husband. She clasped the big cookpot of rice for lunch on her lap with one hand and her husband's belt with the other. Sofia sat on an extension bar at the back, holding onto her mother. Javi, his next younger brother, Diego, and Bel and I spent the ten sol on a bicycle taxi or walked.

They took us to their farm a couple of times, and it was an oasis moment in the desert of city living for us. To actually see something green and be able to eat avocado or a fruit off the tree was so nice, since I was struggling with the food. They ate rice twice a day, which I could handle if it was just rice. But they always put something with the rice, and it was so spicy it made me ill. I tried to explain that I just wanted rice, but it seemed it was incomprehensible to them to feed me only rice. Telling them it was too spicy didn't work, as they didn't think it was spicy at all. Breakfast was the only meal I could eat. We had a cup of hot evaporated milk with flakes of oatmeal and a roll with avocado. I loved that meal. The other two gave me stomach cramps for hours and occasionally physical illness.

Soon their dog learned to sit under the table beside me, as I would slip whatever I could to him when no one was looking. Belinda would always try the food first and then look at me and either give a slight nod or shake of her head. This would let me know if it was something I could handle or if I should try to dispose of it somehow. I always carried a rag in my pocket to try and hide some food if the dog wasn't available.

One time I outsmarted myself. Bel had given a vigorous shake to her head just as Elena headed over to the stove. I quickly palmed the food and slipped it to the dog. Mission accomplished. When Elena returned and saw my plate was empty, a beatific smile spread across her face.

"Bueno, bueno!" She quickly grabbed the cooking pot and plopped a double portion on my plate. Belinda snorted and quickly turned it into a cough at the look of frustration that crossed my face.

We usually had a two-hour period between the Sunday morning service and the call for lunch. Many times we tortured ourselves recounting all the good food Belinda had at her graduation.

One day after we'd been there a month or so, we wandered into one of the little shops. I was gazing at the displays when suddenly an elbow jammed into my midriff.

"Ooff! Whatcha' do that for?" I grumbled as I looked at Belinda. She had fastened her gaze on a spot above the storekeeper's head.

"Look on the top shelf!"

I followed her gaze and spied what she had seen.

"Oh, my goodness, a can of Del Monte peaches!" I felt the saliva pool in my mouth just looking at that can.

"That's the first American food I've seen in over a month!" Bel mouthed the words with awe.

"Shall we buy it?" She gave me such a look of disdain that I rephrased my words. "I meant, let's buy it!" I pointed to the shopkeeper and then at the shelf. He looked at the can, then at us, and shook his head and brushed a hand as if to say, "No, you don't want that."

When we kept nodding and pointing, he finally got his step stool, climbed up, and lifted down the dust-encrusted can. Brushing it off with his apron, he set it in front of us.

We nearly fell over when we realized it would cost us $6.00 for the one can. (This was at the time when they were only 67 cents a can in Canada.) We were being ripped off royally, but we didn't care. We wanted those peaches!

Triumphantly we arrived home with our prize, only to discover our second problem. These Peruvians didn't have a can opener; they never needed one.

We'd invested so much money and effort into this treat there was no way we were going to admit failure. We headed to our concrete bedroom and started looking through our supplies. I came up with my fingernail clippers. By taking turns and stopping to apply adhesive bandages on the cuts the ragged metal gave our fingers (thankfully we'd brought a very good amount of medical supplies with us), an hour later we had pried open that lid far enough to get to the peaches. There was blood from the cuts on our fingers mingled in with the juice of the peaches, but never did a dessert taste so good!

I also found a store that sold chocolate. It was quite bitter, but I found that if I ate a chocolate bar after each meal, it managed to alleviate some of the sting and burn my mouth was enduring from the spicy meals.

They had some special food for special times, so it wasn't all bad, but I certainly had moments that were tough on my digestion.

Our doctor in Canada had also warned us that the water in Peru might not be good, so we should boil everything before we drank it. That sounded good, but when you're living in someone's home and can't communicate with them, it's easier said than done. This mom had only two small burners to cook meals for eight people, so she couldn't understand why we'd waste gas heating water. She kept trying to give us tea if we asked to boil the water. So we finally gave up the attempt. We'd fill our water bottles and let them sit for several days. By then you could see little things in the bottom of our bottles, so we'd tip them carefully and just sip the top two-thirds off and then dump the rest. That water might also have contributed to some of my stomach issues, but Belinda didn't seem to get as sick as I did over things, so we weren't sure.

Chapter 13

Once we started with school, we soon developed a routine. We had school from 8:00 to 10:30 with students. Then I gave Javi a private lesson until noon. Bel used that time to do our laundry, work on Spanish, help in a class, et cetera. We had an hour for lunch, and then we were with students from 1:00 to 5:00. Once they left, we held ESL (English as a Second Language) for adults until 6:00. We were supposed to assist with the ESL but ended up in charge, as the teacher insisted on sitting with his students. Javi explained he was too embarrassed to teach in front of real English speakers.

They were long days for us, but with over a hundred students attending, they had to split the school sessions to be able to seat everyone. The younger students came from 8:00 to 12:00, while the high school was from 1:00 to 5:00. By the time the adults left at 6:00, Bel and I wanted nothing more than to just sit in our bedrooms. But Spanish people believe in hospitality. Sitting alone or leaving the youth functions in the evening to go to bed early was not acceptable. Javi tried to explain that they would feel we were mad at them if we left. But our brains were so tired of trying to listen, function, and comprehend all day long, we weren't always in the mood for "fun" after the day was done.

I had considered myself to be a "people person." Being in Peru taught me that although I enjoy fun and games and people, I'm actually a loner. I can be the life of the party, but I desperately need my space and my alone time as well. The Lord was certainly stretching me as I had to adapt to this culture of togetherness.

Not that I didn't enjoy some of the things we did. There were a few girls our age who seemed very nice. However, because Javi was the only one who could speak much English, out of necessity the majority of our time was spent with him and his friends. His younger brother, Diego, was an amazing musician. The church had an old piano, which was quite out of tune, but Diego could make beautiful music come out of it. I had brought my flute along, and when he realized that, we became good friends, although he was shy and it was difficult to get him to ask me to play with him the first time.

There was a knock on my door. When I opened it, Diego stood there.

"Senorita, you like …"

"Yes?"

"Maybe you want …"

"Yes."

"No problem." He turned to walk away.

"Diego, what's up?"

He half-turned around. "You probably not want anyhow."

"Not want what?"

"I no bother you." He turned and took a few steps. I ran after him and grabbed his arm.

"Now I'm curious! What don't I want? I'm not doing anything right now."

"Really?"

"Yes!"

"I hear you haf musica?" He mimed playing a flute.

"Si! I love music, and that instrument could fit in my suitcase."

"I play, too—piano."

Suddenly it clicked. "Are you going to play piano now and want me to play with you?"

He turned red, stared at the floor, and then nodded. I whacked him on the back and he glanced up in surprise. "I'd love to! Thanks so much for asking."

That was the start of one of the biggest stress-relievers for me. We played many of the hymns together. When people found out that Bel and I loved singing, many requests for duets came. Occasionally we turned them into quartets with Javi and his friend Pedro. I found it terribly hard to learn Spanish; I even struggled as a child to speak English, let alone learn another language. But singing in Spanish was not a problem, as the hymns were all familiar tunes, and mispronunciation wasn't as noticeable.

Many special events in the church found us doing songs at them. If Belinda and I sang duets, we'd also put in English songs, which they liked as well.

The church services were hard on both Javi and myself. We'd sit close together and he'd try to translate in a whisper. But he struggled with how to change the words, and then he wanted me to fill in. But listening to broken English whispered beside you was such a brain strain that it often gave me a headache by the end of the service.

I was finally able to convince him that we were fine with just sitting through the service and listening to the Spanish. That way I could listen, try and pick out some words, and then let my mind wander so my brain could rest.

The services were well attended. They had around 250 people. That many showed up for Sunday morning services, Sunday evening services, and Wednesday evening Bible study. About half of them also showed up for the Friday evening youth group events. It made me wonder why church was so important to them while our country struggled to get people in. Belinda and I discussed it one day.

"Do you notice how nobody misses a single church service?" I tossed the comment out as we headed to our room after one service.

"Yeah. It's so weird. At home, just getting everyone to church Sunday morning is a big deal." Bel flopped on her bed.

"It's kind of embarrassing."

Bel flipped over to look at me. "What do you mean by that?"

"They seem so much more spiritual than we are. They're so enthusiastic about being at every service it makes me feel ashamed."

We pondered that a bit. Bel scrunched her nose. "But have you noticed that's the only place they seem to go. Church and work."

"Hmmm, you do have a point."

"Our country is so busy with sports, musical events, and all kinds of different functions. We go somewhere different every night. By Sunday we're tired."

I laughed.

"What's so funny?"

"On the humourous side, you have to admit we have to go various places for our entertainment. Here you can go to church and have entertainment all in one spot."

Bel's eyes rolled. "I'm not sure setting your hair on fire is exactly 'entertainment.' And I definitely don't want another lantern explosion. That scared me half-to-death!"

Since the power was off more than it was on, we had a few learning curves in living by candlelight much of the time. Once in a while a lady would come into the bathroom and clean the floor. She had just finished cleaning the place when the power went off. As we lit our candles to enter the bathroom, I opened the door, and the smell hit us.

Bel choked. "What is that?"

I held a finger under my nose. "Whew. I think it's kerosene. She had what looked like a gas can with her stick and rags." We walked farther in and Bel leaned forward to set her candle on the ledge above the sink.

My fingers plucked the candle from her hand. "Ah Bel, just let me hold these while you go to the bathroom. Then you hold them for me."

"Why?"

"Bel!" I frowned at her. "Think. Fire from candle, kerosene …"

"Ah!" Bel leaned forward and puffed out both candles. We plunged into a pitch-black opaqueness.

"Bel! Why did you do that? We're in the middle of the room. How are we going to find our way out?"

Out of the inky darkness I heard her voice. "I have no desire to go 'boom' in the bathroom." My imagination took flight as I thought about that phrase and I started giggling.

"What's so funny? We have enough other ways to get blown up. Why risk it here?"

"Oh Bel, just think about it. 'Boom in the Bathroom.' What a story title!"

We both started laughing. When we managed to control ourselves, I continued. "At least neither of us is scared of the dark. But, man, I have no idea which way the door is."

Bel reached out her hand, which of course I didn't see. "Here, take my hand. If we hang on to each other and slowly move around, we've got to hit a wall eventually. Then we can follow along it until we find the door."

It took a bit, and a few bumps and bruises, but we eventually got out of the bathroom.

I grinned at her. "I know I get lost easily, but that's the first time I've ever been lost in a bathroom—but at least I didn't go 'boom!'" That set us to laughing again.

The first time the power went off in the evening service, a few men started two kerosene lanterns. One was placed on a stool on either side of the pulpit, and Javi's dad just kept preaching. Suddenly there was a huge hissing sound, a boom, and the lantern became ablaze with flames. Bel and I both shrieked, but Javi Sr. didn't even stop preaching. Another man grabbed a big old iron bucket, kicked the stool out from under the fiery blaze, and clamped the bucket over the whole mess. With lack of oxygen, the fire was soon out.

My hair-on-fire incident occurred partly because of my poor posture. We sat on straight wooden benches with backs that came up to our shoulder blades. When the power was off, the two lanterns only lit the preacher's pulpit. The rest of the crowd simply pulled candles, or candle parts, from their pockets. One person lit his candle and it was passed around to light other people's candles until there was enough light for the service. What I didn't realize was that instead of just holding their candles, some people would tip them over the back of the pew in front of them, let the melted wax drip onto the wood, and then place their candle in it to secure it to the bench.

As we were listening one evening, I slumped back against the hard wooden bench. I smiled and Belinda noticed and asked, "What are you smiling about?"

"It must finally be warming up here in Peru."

"What makes you say that?"

"I'm finally feeling warmer. Who would ever have guessed being in the tropics would be so bone-chilling cold!" I rubbed my hands together.

"Yeah, next time you tell me you're taking me close to the equator, remember to check if there are mountains and altitudes so we know to bring warm clothes instead of beach clothes!"

I sighed. "I know. Sorry. Live and learn."

Her mouth pouted. "As long as we don't freeze to death so we can't live to learn!" She paused. "Do you smell something?"

I crinkled my nose. "Something always smells around here."

"No, something smells like it's burning." She glanced behind her. "A-a-a-h! Stacy! Your hair!"

No sooner had the words left her mouth than the man behind me started whacking me with the hymnal.

"Ouch! What's going on?" I twisted away in anger, and another person grabbed my shoulders to hold me still as the man whacked a couple more times. Belinda's eyes looked horrified, yet she giggled.

"I'm being attacked and you're laughing?"

She shrugged. "Your hair was on fire. The guy behind you had put his candle on the pew, and you leaned back into it."

The man finished his swats, smiled at me, and returned to listening to the sermon. Not a lot fazed these people. I smiled a thank you back and tried to remain upright for the rest of the service.

The hair was not too badly damaged, and I just trimmed the singed stuff away. The second time I caught my hair on fire, I did more damage to it and had to cut a bit off of the bottom.

We were in our bedroom and suddenly gunshots were fired. We stared at each other.

"Do you think they're shooting at us?" the quaver in Belinda's voice matched the quiver in my legs.

"I hope not. We took down our Canadian flag we had hanging in our window, like Javi asked us to do."

"Yeah, when he said that could be seen from the window and could create some trouble, I couldn't believe it. But that was real gunfire. What are they shooting?"

"I'll see if I can see what's going on." I stood up and moved toward the window.

"You can't stand in front of the window! They can easily shoot you that way." Belinda's voice rose a notch.

"I'll stick the candle in the window and then climb on the counter and look out the top of the window." I crawled on my hands and knees over to the frame and shakily shoved the candle onto the ledge. I dropped flat on the floor and waited. More shots sounded, but nothing came through our window. I slid over to the wall, clambered up onto the counter, and edged next to the window. Holding my breath, I cautiously tipped my head upside-down and peered out. Several men with machine guns were in the street below with their backs to me. They were randomly shooting into the ground or the air.

"Hey, it's not us personally. They're just shooting—probably to scare people." I heaved a sigh of relief but jerked in surprise as Belinda shrieked.

"A-a-a-h!"

"What?"

"Your hair!"

I glanced down and realized by turning my head upside-down, my braid had slipped out and fallen into the burning candle.

"A-a-h!" I hopped to the ground while Belinda, with great presence of mind, grabbed a jar of water and dropped my flaming braid into it.

"W-h-e-w! Thanks! Have I ever told you how glad I am you came along?"

Belinda dropped to the bed. "Yeah, right."

I jerked my head to stare at her. "What's that supposed to mean?"

"There's no point in me being here." Her foot moodily kicked at a dust bunny. "All I do is trail you around, do oddball things, and scrub my hands raw doing our laundry."

I sat beside her. "Remember how I was hesitant about having you come?"

Her head bobbed once. "Yup. I should have listened to you."

"I'm so glad you didn't. God knew how desperately I'd need someone here to help me keep my sanity."

"I'm not doing anything you couldn't do for yourself."

I took her by the shoulders and looked her in the eyes. "Belinda, God knew I wouldn't have made it through this without someone else here. It's why He put that thought in your parents' minds and hearts. Just the need to speak to someone who can understand English is a huge help. And having you next to me helps mitigate the fear of whether we're going to survive these guerrillas or not. Never, ever doubt that you're doing what God wants."

"I'll try to remember."

"And I'll try to thank you more often."

"How about thanking me by letting me have first bath all the time."

"I'm not that thankful!" I grinned and flopped onto the bed.

Because of the power outages, the cistern in the courtyard was the main source of water. We dreaded the shower—when the water was running. The mountain water runoff was so cold that our lips sometimes had a blueish tinge by the time we had showered. So when we found a small, red plastic dishpan, it became the most important item in our room. We lugged water from the cistern across the courtyard, through the church, up the stairs, and into our bedroom. We waited three days and set candles burning next to it in the misbegotten hope it would warm the water. Then we tossed a coin to see who got to wash her hair first. When one was done, the other person washed her hair. After that, one of us bathed, and then the other. When we finished our bath, we used the water to wash our undergarments and small things. Once we had those up on the roof to try to dry, we used the final round of water to clean the room. Hauling water by bucketful a distance made us use every drop well.

We tried to take these sponge baths once a week yet always felt gritty. However, the people around us were always sniffing us and saying we smelled "boo-ti-ful." We considered ourselves tough Canadians so couldn't understand how we could hear Javi whistle when he'd take a shower in his house, while we shivered and moaned.

One day Belinda burst into the room. "I don't believe it! You'll never guess!"

I looked up from my diary. "What?"

"You know how Javi whistles when he showers, and we think he's crazy?"

"Yeah, so what?"

"Well, I actually went into the washroom inside their house—they have an electric shower!"

"A-n-n-d-d?" I didn't get the point.

"Electricity—when the power is on, they have hot water!"

I threw the diary down. "You're kidding? And they never told us?"

"No. I'm fuming. We've been crying in our ice shower in the courtyard while he was whistling in his electric warm water."

We immediately asked if we could try their shower. Belinda had first chance at it. She came back smiling and said, "Well, it's only lukewarm, but look at my mouth. It didn't turn blue."

The next day I asked to give it a go, as the power was on. Standing there with the trickle of warmish water felt good, but then I reached out my wet hand to turn off the metal tap. Zzzzitttt! A massive shock ran through my arm. It was so strong I couldn't open my fingers to let the tap go. Another jolt of electricity ran through me. I don't know how long I would have stood being electrocuted but the power suddenly went off. I was never so grateful for a power outage. I was able to release my hand and shakily towel off.

When I returned upstairs, Bel smiled at me. "Nice, wasn't it?"

I flexed my fingers thoughtfully. "Not sure the warmer water was worth being electrocuted."

She flipped over on the bed and stared at me. "You didn't grab the metal tap while you were wet, did you?"

"How else was I to turn the water off?"

She laughed. I scowled. "Don't see anything funny here."

She tried to sober up. "You're the teacher, and you can't figure out wet body plus metal tap equals volts? For goodness' sakes, step out of the shower, towel off, then use edge of towel to turn tap off. It's just a tiny snap then." As my scowl deepened, she laughed some more. "You honestly never thought about that, did you? Guess it is a good thing I came along with you. You can be so oblivious about some things."

Belinda used the electric shower periodically when she could, but I'd gotten such a severe jolt that I just decided I'd rather cry and turn blue than have that voltage running through me again.

Chapter 14

Although we were from Canada and used to cold weather, we had come prepared for the tropics. I hadn't done my research well. I'd just seen that we were close to the equator and forgot that the altitude would also make a difference. When we arrived, Javi also told us that they were having a record cold winter. So the light clothes we brought, while actually nice when it came to washing and rinsing and wringing out by hand, were not good when it came to living in a cold, damp concrete building. I had brought only one sweatshirt along—just in case. I ended up wearing it constantly during the day, and at bedtime rolled it up for a pillow. Since Bel had her pillow, she gave me a hard time about my pillow-less state, since it had been so hotly debated whether to bring it or not.

We were never sure if it was the light clothing or a new culture, but Peru was a bit hard on our health. The roof of the church was a flat slab of concrete, so we hung our clothes up there. It took three days to try to get them to dry in the damp humidity there, and then we'd bring them to bed and sleep on them for a night to warm them up enough to finish drying so we could wear them. That could also have contributed to the nasty colds we came down with. Trying to get cold medication to help us recover was a struggle. Javi took us to the drugstore, but it was a building that was kept locked with bars at all the windows. You stood outside and requested Advil; after some time, the druggist would open a small slot. You placed your money in it, and then a tiny envelope would appear through the slot. Inside would be two pills. We tried countless times to get the man to give us a dozen so we wouldn't have to trek back to the store twice a day, but that's all he would dispense at a time. We hadn't brought tons of cold medications with us so had to learn that "when in Rome, do as the Romans do."

The colds were something I just learned to live with. To a certain extent I learned to live with the stomach cramps and occasional bouts of vomiting that came with eating food my stomach found too spicy. People were so gracious about wanting to give us their best. I felt terrible that I couldn't explain that it wasn't their food but my stomach that was the problem. Of course, moments when we saw a chicken foot in the soup, we managed to pass the bowl to the next person. After we heard guinea pig was considered a delicacy, we decided not to ask what we were eating anymore.

But of greater concern to me health-wise was my big toe. I don't know what happened, but one day I realized my toe hurt. Belinda commented on it as we walked along.

"You seem to be limping. What's wrong?"

"I don't know. My toe hurts."

"Maybe you stubbed it."

"Yeah, these streets are awfully rough."

I didn't think much about it, but the limp turned to burning, and the burning to downright pain. Since I was wearing socks 24/7, I didn't think much about it. But one morning I went to put my shoe on.

"A-w-w-w."

Belinda turned around. "What's going on?"

"I don't know. I can't put my shoe on. It's killing my foot."

"Let's take a look."

When we pulled my sock off, I gaped in amazement. The toe was about three times its normal size and visibly throbbing. Belinda whistled.

"Whoa, that doesn't look good. How could you not have noticed this before?"

My fear made my voice tremble. "I told you my foot hurt."

"This isn't 'hurt.' This is serious. Do you think we should try to go to the hospital?"

I jerked my foot back. "Are you kidding? If they only give us two pills for a nasty cold, what do you think they'd do for a bad toe?"

Belinda grinned for a moment. "I don't know. Cut it off, maybe?"

"That's not funny, and who knows—maybe that's not far off. I'm not going to a hospital here."

Belinda's face grew serious. "Stacy, I'm not a medical person, but that doesn't look like anything to joke about."

"Where are the alcohol swabs? Let's try that." I rooted around in the bag of First Aid supplies.

After wiping my toe and area with the alcohol, I switched over to my sandals. When we were out on the streets, we usually wore our running shoes to protect our feet from the dirt and germs in the roads, but I could only get something open-toed on.

Several days later, we noticed the red streaks. Belinda got very worried.

"Stacy, this is beyond serious. Red streaks are major infections. Just rubbing your toe isn't doing anything. Hand me one of the needles."

When we'd gotten our shots, the doctor had told us to pack syringes and rubbing alcohol in our supplies, as some countries reuse their needles. We didn't think we'd need a syringe for anything but had brought two packs in just in case.

"What are you going to do?"

"If we squeeze the alcohol from the swabs into a needle, I can shoot it into your toe. That's got to do more good than just rubbing the outside. The infection is internal. You don't want to lose your toe, do you?"

I weakly grimaced. "With the pain it's giving me right now, that's not sounding like a bad option." She glared and I shrunk back. "Okay, okay. Bad joke. Hand me a swab."

It took us all afternoon to carefully open the swabs and squish out some drops of alcohol from each into the needles.

"Bel."

"Hmm?" She mumbled as her hands concentrated on holding the needle steady.

"Next time, let's bring a bottle of rubbing alcohol instead of swabs. This is very tedious."

She huffed. "Next time don't do whatever you did to make your toe like this." She tapped the row of needles we'd filled. "I think there's enough in there now." She picked up my foot. "So where do you think is the best place to jab this into?"

I scanned my foot. "How about right where the red streaks start?"

"Okay." She paused and then stabbed the needle into my foot.

"A-h-h-h!" I let out an involuntary kick, and she fell over.

"Hey! What did you do that for?"

I glared at her. "I didn't mean to; I couldn't help it."

We stared at the foot. After a few minutes, Bel sighed. "Well, I don't see any change. Let's try the next needle. I'll put it in the end of the toe. Maybe needles from both sides will do something."

I whimpered. "I hate needles."

She picked up the syringe. "So don't look this time."

Another jab, another kick.

"Ouch. Stop that. I'm trying to help!"

"Sorry. I can't help it. It's an involuntary reaction."

"So flip over on your stomach."

"Why?"

"Just do it." I flipped, and then next thing I knew, Bel was sitting on top of me. With me yelling and she jabbing, she emptied all the syringes into various parts of my toe. When they were all gone, she rolled off me.

"Well, I give up. I don't know what else to do."

I wiped the tears streaming down my face with the edge of my sleeve. "I would have preferred you to give up a few needles ago! Look at my toe. With all that alcohol in there, now it's four times the proper size."

Belinda giggled. "Do you think you can get drunk if you've taken in too much alcohol through the toe end of your body?"

I threw her pillow at her but had to laugh at the picture that thought brought to mind.

The next morning, we sat up in bed.

"Let's look at your toe and see if anything happened." Belinda pulled at my sock. We both sighed in disappointment as the red-streaked, throbbing toe showed up.

"All that pain for nothing," I sighed as I leaned over and gently pushed on the nail.

W-h-o-o-o-s-h. We both shrieked as a massive glob of the grossest green and yellow slimeball shot out from under the nail and splattered on the wall beside us. A vile stench made us gag.

"Gross! What was that?" Bel grabbed for her pillow and buried her nose in it.

I stared in horrified fascination as the goop slowly slithered down the wall. "Phee-uw! But how cool was that?" I pushed on my nail again. *Whooosh.* Another slimeball, a bit smaller, shot out and joined the first one.

"Aah, the smell!" Bel gagged. "How can it shoot out of your toe like that?"

I shrugged. "You poked enough holes in my toe with all those needles you jabbed into me, so probably through one of those. But look at my toe. It's not so big!" Another two pushes on the nail removed the rest of the gunk that was still hiding in there. We wrapped a couple of alcohol swabs around the nail and bandaged them onto the toe for the day.

Within a couple of days, the red streaks had disappeared and my toe was feeling much better. Belinda couldn't help crowing. "Well, guess I make a pretty good doctor, eh?"

I groaned. "Don't get a big head. I can't say much for your bedside manner. Sitting on top of your patient, hmm? Besides, God needs the credit for this. We didn't have a clue what we were doing."

Belinda sobered up. "Amen to that. I was so scared I was going to lose you, and I didn't know how I'd survive without you."

I smiled at her. "It's a two-way street, gal. And I you. I've been praying that if one of us has to die, that it'll be me. I sure don't want to have to go back and face your parents without you."

Tears glistened in her eyes. "I've been praying the very same thing."

I stuck out my hand. "Well, let's make a pact. By God's grace, let's plan that both of us can climb on that plane come September 12." We shook hands and tried to leave the matter with God.

Chapter 15

Fear. It was a word I hadn't known could exist in the way we were experiencing it in Peru. In some ways being oblivious to the news kept us from knowing how bad things were becoming.

The first reality check came to me the day we were on a bus with Javi, Diego, and his friend Chencho. Chencho and I hit it off right from the beginning. He was a fourteen-year-old "cool dude." He was also taller than me and loved that fact. Since Belinda was five feet, and I was five-three, we were surprised to realize that we were as tall as many of the Peruvian men, and much taller than most women. It was great to feel so tall.

As we were on the bus, a military-style vehicle passed by. Soon shouts of soldiers and screams of women filtered back to us. I looked at Javi, who shrugged.

"Right now, because of the terrorist onslaught, soldiers are desperately needed. So the army takes guys if they can't prove they have already served or that they're under eighteen."

"How do you 'show' this?"

Chencho shrugged. "We're supposed to carry papers at all times to show our age and whether we have done military duty yet." His nonchalant attitude aroused my suspicions.

"And where are you carrying these papers right now?"

He grinned. "I don't need them. I'm faster than the soldiers. Twice now they've tried to take me, but I managed to escape."

Diego frowned. "You've been lucky, but one of these days they'll get you, and then how will your mother feel when you don't come home?"

I looked at Javi. He nodded. "I have my papers here." He tapped his jacket pocket. "But it's true. If sons suddenly disappear, most families expect the army has them. Once you've served two years, you receive a paper for that. If you don't keep that paper on you as proof, then you can end up serving another two years."

I glared at Chencho. "You make sure you start carrying those papers." He grinned and shrugged.

Not long after that, the five of us were again on a bus headed home from some sightseeing and shopping. In our area, bus seats were a luxury, not a requirement. If you got to sit in one, fine, or you could share your seat with a few others. If not, you stood in the aisles. There seemed to be no limit to the amount of people or livestock they'd crowd on a bus. Chickens often came along, or guinea pigs. I think many people bought their meat live and carted it home with the rest of their groceries.

The five of us were crammed into three seats near the back of the bus, swaying to the jolting of the road, when the bus came to an abrupt halt. Both the front and back doors flipped open and several soldiers with machine guns jumped in. After shouting in Spanish, they started looking at papers the men were pulling out of their pockets. I turned to look at Chencho. He had a "deer in the headlights" look. Belinda clutched my arm.

"What are we going to do? We can't let them take Chencho. He's only fourteen." I glanced at the soldiers, who were still several seats away from us. I slid my eyes over to Chencho, jerked my head down, and pointed a finger. He did the most gracious spaghetti-noodle slide down to the floor without making a sound. Since I was wearing a broomstick skirt, I was able to gradually slide off the seat, sit on the curled-up Chencho and cover him with my skirt. Bel caught on and quickly slid over to fill our shared seat, using the bags of stuff we had bought to help cover the small amount of space left on the seat.

We weren't a minute too soon. As one soldier yanked a protesting man off the bus, another turned his attention to our seats. His eyes widened as he saw our white skin, and he shouted something. Another soldier quickly spun around, raised his machine gun, and pointed it a few inches from my stomach.

Javi quickly handed his papers to the man and spoke in rapid Spanish. The soldier poked me with his gun and said something. I was pretty sure I was being told to stand up, but I just smiled my widest smile I could muster.

"Please, sir, I think you want me to stand, but I can't because I'm hiding a boy under my skirt. Since he's only fourteen, you really don't want him."

Belinda went into a violent coughing fit, while both Diego and Javi stared at me like I'd sprouted horns. I looked down at the ground, and to my horror, I saw three feet sticking out from under my skirt. I casually drew one of mine back farther under the skirt while praying fervently the guy wouldn't notice I had two left feet and one foot was bigger than the other.

The soldier poked me one more time and I groaned and made gagging sounds. It wasn't dishonest; I was so scared, I felt like I could easily throw up. I could hear Javi making comments.

"La nina es poco loco y enferma." I knew "poco loco" meant a little crazy and wasn't complimentary, but the men, after reaching out, pinching my white skin, and checking their fingers, moved on.

Belinda gave a shaky laugh. "Javi's right. You are poco loco, telling those men you were hiding Chencho from them." She extended a hand to help me up. I was grateful for the support, as I wasn't sure my legs would hold me.

"Since I knew they wouldn't understand my English, I was just being honest." As I squished back into my seat with Bel, Chencho unfolded himself from the floor, stood up, and grinned.

"See? No problemo!"

A rush of anger roared through me, and I grabbed him by the shirt. "Don't you ever do that to me again. You carry your papers when you're with us, you hear?"

He uncurled my shaking fingers. "Si, si. Don't worry." He looked puzzled that I was angry.

I heaved a sigh. "The things I do for students."

Bel smirked. "Was this worse than riding that horse when Faith managed to pass two algebra tests without failing? Or how about standing on your head when Kent got 100% in his science?"

"They were maybe close seconds." We grinned as the boys looked puzzled. "Inside joke."

Javi's eyes lit up. "Joke? I love jokes."

We groaned. We knew. We'd spent hours trying to explain cultural English jokes to him.

As time went on, we weren't sure if we should be more scared of the guerrillas or the police. The guerrillas terrified me because, although I could handle dying, the thought of being taken hostage and/or tortured as a political incident was a huge fear. However, the police were also scary due to the fact that we terrified them with our white skin and didn't know what they'd do to us. With everyone living in fear and worry about the opposing faction, by July 17, Javi's dad told us not to leave the house without one of them.

"Terrorists have blown up some buses," Javi Sr. told us via Javi's translation. "Unfortunately, there are rumours that white activists are helping, so the police are on the lookout for any strange, white people."

Bel and I inched closer to each other. "But we don't have anything to do with it," I protested. Bel nodded in agreement.

"Stacy can't even start a fire for camping, let alone make a bomb."

"Six hundred kilos of dynamite have been stolen, and the bombing is getting nearer, so strangers are going to be the first to get questioned." Javi finished translating and then looked at our scared faces. His dad spoke again. "But Dad says don't worry. If God wants us dead, we'll be dead. Otherwise, we won't."

I gritted my teeth and sent a quick prayer upward.

God, what he says is true, and I know that, but if You wanted us dead, couldn't You just have done that back in Canada? I really, really don't want to die down here.

Keep holding on to Me, my child.

I will, Lord, but really—why do I have to go through this?

Having this experience will help you to help others.

Yeah, IF I live through it.

I did not promise there'd be no trouble or loss but that I would be with you through the valley of the shadow of death.

It'd be really nice to know if this is just going to be a shadow, or ...

Grace for the moment, child. Not for the day, or week, or future.

Bel and I decided it was time to make the trek to the phone company and see if we could make contact with home. Javi and Diego walked the blocks with us that evening. Suddenly, Bel grabbed my arm.

"Stacy, very slowly turn your head and look up on the roof of that house. There's a man with a gun." Her sibilant whisper had me jerking, but her increased grip slowed my reaction. I gradually glanced around and saw she was right. A machine gun pointing down at us tracked our movements.

"Javi, are we going to get shot?"

He looked up and then just kept walking. "No problem. He's just a guard making sure that building stays safe."

After the stress of that silent walk, we were doubly disappointed when we spent an hour waiting for a call that wouldn't go through. On the way home I tucked my arm through Belinda's.

"In some ways I suppose it's a good thing we've only been able to call twice."

"What makes you say that? I want desperately to talk to my family."

"I do, too. But my folks lost a son almost a year ago. If they knew what we were going through, that wouldn't be good."

Bel puffed out a long breath. "Yeah, Mom would freak if she could see us right now."

"Bel, to my dying day, I'll be grateful that you're here with me right now."

"Don't say that!"

I looked at her in amazement. "Why not? I mean that. This is the first time I've had someone with me on a journey, and I don't think I could have done this without you."

"No, I meant don't say 'til my dying day.' That day is looking very close right about now!"

We both laughed. I think we developed a type of "gallows humour" to help us vent our emotions at the sights, sounds, and smells that were bombarding our senses.

After a moment she continued. "It certainly is easier on the pocketbook, too. I had to pay $40 for that last seven-minute call."

"Ouch!"

"Yeah."

To our amazement, the next morning at breakfast, Javi Sr. nodded, smiled, and spoke to his son. Javi turned to us. "Dad said to take the day off and go to Lima."

Belinda smiled back. "Why?" I was equally curious.

"You are seeing Peru at its worst. We want to take you sightseeing to show you there are some amazing things about our country."

Bel and I looked at each other and grinned with delight. As soon as breakfast was over, we headed to our bedroom to get ready to leave.

Chapter 16

Our sightseeing trip was amazing—not least of all because we survived it. When we arrived in Lima, the power was off, so no streetlights were operating. To begin with, Peruvian driving is nothing like the strictly regulated Canadian driving rules we were accustomed to following. With the stoplights not working, it became a madhouse of "may the best man win." After the first few narrow escapes trying to cross the streets on foot with Javi nonchalantly swerving in and out and sometimes even over vehicles, I looked at Belinda.

"Are we playing chicken or suicide here?"

She gave her wicked-witch cackle that she reserved for special occasions. "A bit of both, I think. This is better than any West Edmonton Mall ride, and it's free!" With that, she darted after Javi.

I moaned. "I forgot how much you love carnival rides. The worse they are, the better you like them. Hey—wait for me!" I tore after them the best I could. By the end of the day, I felt quite pleased with myself. Despite my balance issues, I had only torn the edge of my skirt in some spots from hooking on bumpers and banged both knees against the front of a few cars. My elbow had connected against a few hoods, but I was all in one piece. That was also due to the fact that Bel and Javi managed to pull and push me through the worst spots.

We did our best to ignore the soldiers and guns that were everywhere. This was our "fun" day, and we were going to enjoy it to the hilt. We went to a castle at the edge of the Pacific Ocean. It was in semi-ruins because of its age, but it was very interesting to wander through it and imagine life so many centuries ago.

A sixteenth-century Franciscan monastery was amazing in a different way. The monastery was impressive, but then we were asked if we wanted to tour the catacombs. My history-loving imagination perked up.

"From the Spanish Inquisition?"

"Yes."

Bel nudged me. "What's that?"

"A time when Christians and others were persecuted if they dared to have an opinion that differed from what was allowed. Because of torture and death, many ran to the catacombs to hide and lived that way. I knew there were catacombs in Italy, but I hadn't realized they had them here."

When we paid to take that tour, I didn't realize how real our experience would be. Because the power was off, there were no lights in the catacombs. The guide had a flashlight, but that was it. So the guide went first and we followed single file. I had said that I didn't want to hear the tour, as I knew some of the terrible things that were done, but Javi and Bel were interested. Therefore, I went last. I didn't realize how narrow, winding, damp, and dark some of those narrow tunnels would be. As fourth in line, the flashlight was merely a speck of light far in front. The darkness could be felt, it was so heavy, and my claustrophobia kicked in. I also kept stumbling in the dark. Bumping against cold, slimy walls was making my balance very off-key.

I grabbed the back of Bel's jacket.

"What's up?" Her whisper echoed eerily in the tunnel.

"I'm having trouble walking. I can't see, can't keep my balance, and can't breathe."

I heard her speak forward to Javi. "Is this going to get more narrow? Stacy's having trouble."

He spoke to the guide and then responded. "We're almost through the worst of it. We'll soon be in the big cavern."

Sure enough, within minutes the corridor widened, and soon we were all able to stand side by side. The guide pulled out a candle, lit a lantern, and then went around this underground cave lighting lanterns strategically placed in the vast openness in which we found ourselves.

As the light flickered against the dripping walls, my eyes popped.

"Whooo, Belinda, what have we gotten into?"

She stepped close and whispered. "I feel like I've been transported into some weird nightmarish movie." I nodded and together we slowly moved farther into the chambers. In some spots there were long, narrow trenches with chains and metal balls plunked sporadically in them. Bones and skulls were sprawled around. The guide beckoned us to the centre pit. Looking down into the huge circular well, we saw leg bones and arm bones in a concentric circle in the centre, with skulls circling the outer edge inside the well.

We looked at the guide. "What is this?"

He said, "History shows that many Christians and poor people came and lived out their lives here. Others who were tortured and escaped made their way here. The chains and the other instruments were taken off here. This well is estimated to be fifteen metres deep and nine metres wide. A few decades ago, when this area was discovered, archeologists asked permission to come in and examine the bones for better understanding of the history of this time and place. So when they finished, they left the skulls and bones in this neat pattern to show their respect for the dead."

I carefully circled the cavern, looking and remembering things I'd read. The reality of how much Christians were willing to suffer for their faith struck me, and I felt I was such a wimp of a person. Although it was eerie and creepy, it was a good place to realize what some people go through.

Once we were back above ground, I breathed a sigh of relief. Bel looked at me.

"I don't know whether to be horrified or amazed."

"I hear you. What a place!" I paused and a thought struck me. "Wow!"

"Wow, what?"

"What a place to be when the Lord returns again!"

"What on earth are you talking about?"

"Well, the Bible says the dead in Christ shall rise first. Can you imagine being able to be right here at that moment? Whooey—just picture all those bones flying back together! Think they'd have an argument about which arm bone goes to which body?"

Bel grimaced. "You are so weird."

I shrugged. I hadn't meant it in a disrespectful way. I just have a vivid imagination and could visualize that amazing event.

After we left the monastery, we went to a cathedral. It was almost boggling to the brain to go so quickly from the austerity of the monastery and the catacombs to the richness and grandeur of the cathedral. We both felt a bit overwhelmed.

"Why do Peruvians have such stunning cathedrals when so many are so poor."

Our guide heard my question to Javi. "The cathedral is the symbol of God here, and God deserves the best."

Again, that was a concept I hadn't thought about, but it was a very good answer.

Of course, we were taking photos with the good camera as we went along. So when Bel asked me to go stand on the grass in front of a neat place, I simply did. We noticed Javi seemed a bit agitated. Bel finally spoke.

"Javi, what's the problem?"

"Just take the photo and leave."

"Why? Are we doing something wrong?"

He shrugged. When we pestered him, he finally spoke. "Well, it's illegal to stand on that grass. If you get caught you could go to jail."

"A-a-h!" I jumped off the spot. "Why didn't you say so?"

"I didn't want to spoil your photo."

I rolled my eyes. "I could have stood on the concrete in front of the grass. Believe me, I'd rather do that than be hauled into jail!"

"Really?" Bel and I grabbed our heads. We'd had these conversations with Javi before. "You need to tell us what we must know, even if it's not what we wanted to do."

He seemed stunned. "But isn't that rude?"

Bel answered. She had more patience than I did with the diversity in our cultures. "It's more important that we don't do something wrong. We have different ways than Peruvians and may not know what's best. So tell us the truth, not what you think we want to hear."

He agreed to try, and we moved on before I did something else I shouldn't do.

Javi's family did other nice things for us as we were able to amidst the tensions of war. It was a delicate balance, but during our time there we were able to see a few art galleries and museums and spend a weekend with the youth at a Bible camp—with green trees and grass! One of the special times for me was going to an Inca cemetery. We walked through an orange grove, which had the juiciest, warmest oranges that we could pick and eat. But when we left the grove behind, we entered a very bleak, deserty-looking area. The roll and dip of the sand dunes were covered with pockets of odds and ends. Skulls, bones, and broken bits of pottery were scattered all over. I turned to Javi.

"This is such an awesome part of Peru's rich heritage and history. Why is it so desecrated?"

He sighed. "Because the Incas were buried with riches and food for their journey to the next life, grave robbers were a problem. Once they realized they could find gold, silver, and artifacts amongst the dead, well, you see the end result."

I walked over and carefully picked up a tiny skull. I saw a long crack running along the base of it and drew in a sharp breath. Bel joined me.

"What is it?"

I shivered. "Can you believe it? Three thousand years ago, some poor Incan lady lost a child and probably never knew why. Yet here I stand holding this skull realizing this baby probably fell down a set of steps, cracked its skull, and died from internal injuries." I felt such a part of history in that moment.

Chapter 17

My birthday was memorable in both good and horrible ways. I turned twenty-five, and Bel went out of her way to give me a special day. She even convinced the mom to give her a pot of boiled water. When she dragged that up into our bedroom, I was touched.

"Hot water? How? What?"

She poured the water into the ice water already sitting in our little red basin. "This is your twenty-fifth. That's a special birthday, so I figured the best thing I could make happen is a warmish bath for you. Happy birthday!"

I jumped up. "Oooh, Bel! You are the most giving person I've ever seen. A warm bath! Oh-la-la."

She laughed. "Don't make me out to be a hero. You only get it for ten minutes. Then I want a go at it, too!"

That absolutely made my day. But she wasn't finished. While I was giving Javi his English lesson, she persuaded the mom to take her shopping. When I returned to the bedroom, she had a piano jewellery box for me, since I like music, and five roses and one carnation in a vase. At 10:00 a.m., the power had come on and lasted for almost twelve hours. A warm water sponge bath, flowers, and electricity—what more could a person possibly need? I felt blessed beyond compare.

I crawled into bed that evening totally satisfied. Bel wasn't quite.

"I'm sorry."

I turned on my side to face her. "Sorry? What for? You gave me a fantastic day."

"But I tried to get the mom to make you a cake. I guess she didn't get what I wanted."

"Oh Bel, that's fine. This was a wonderful day."

Just then there was a knock on the door. I looked at my watch. It was 9:30 p.m. When we opened it, Diego stood there.

"Vamos. Tu fiesta de cumpleanos." He beckoned us.

Bel laughed. "Maybe she did understand me."

I groaned. "But at 9:30 p.m.? It's bedtime. I'm not a night owl."

She punched my shoulder. "Get dressed. When in Rome …"

So I entered the kitchen to another two hours of party. They went out of their way—balloons, a sign with both the Peruvian and Canadian flag, some fun family games, and our first cake. That turned a bit embarrassing for me. It was a small rectangular cake, longer than wide. After singing to me, the mom gave me the knife and motioned to cut the first piece. With eight of us, I cut a slice about a quarter of the way down and then planned to turn it and cut it in half again. But the mom got a horrified look, quickly took the knife, and proceeded to make seven thin slices across the remaining three-quarters of cake. I tried to show her I wanted to slice the piece I had in half, but she insisted I keep and eat that. I felt mortified at my huge quarter of the cake while everyone nibbled their thin slice, but Bel thought it was hilarious. I have to admit, I loved eating the entire piece. It didn't give me stomach cramps or burn my mouth.

Unfortunately, the joy of the day turned into the terror of the night. Just before midnight, we felt the first bomb go off. The building shook but stayed standing. The constant gunfire almost disturbed us more.

The dad disappeared for a bit and then returned. The terrorists had arrived in our town. Anyone caught walking in the streets was forced to lie face down on the ground. If they stayed still, the guerrillas shot over them, but didn't kill them. Two boys were taken hostage a few blocks from us. Notices were being spray painted on buildings to stay home for two days or risk being shot. Javi's dad tried to reassure us.

"Remember, the Lord is in control. If He wants us to be dead, we'll be with Him." But his eyes and face were so sad as he spoke that I hurt for him and his family. When I said as much to Javi, he almost had tears in his eyes.

"It is a sad, sad time for our country. We have never had this in our city before."

Needless to say, Bel and I didn't sleep much. We gathered our passports, money, and plane tickets and kept them in a bag in case of a quick departure. Then we took turns standing guard while the other rested. Bombs six blocks away just shook our building, but when one exploded a couple of blocks away, that threw us out of the bed. I started one of the most intense yet very short prayers I knew—*Help, Lord!*

After two days, things seemed to settle down, so we were invited to play soccer with another group. It was an hour-long walk to get to their field, but with our "team" chatting as we walked, it went quickly. However, I was downright disgusted when I got there to find that "playing" meant sitting and watching the *boys* play. They were astonished that I'd even consider playing. The girls were simply there to watch and cheer.

I watched and fumed. When they were done, Chencho came to me.

"You think you really could play like that?"

"Yes!" I snapped and turned away. He put a hand on my shoulder and turned me back.

"You strange girl!"

"Ha! Just watch, I'll show you strange!" I huffed and got up.

Chencho laughed. "Hokay—I want to jog home. Think you can keep up?" His eyes twinkled a challenge.

Diego called to Bel. "We'll let her jog home with us—if she can! Are you okay to come home with the kids?"

"Sure, go ahead." She waved us on.

My anger at being excluded from a game I'd walked an hour to play helped me to keep up a very steady pace. Occasionally I had to slow to a walk to catch my breath but then would break into a run again. I couldn't outrun the boys, but they were puffing pretty hard when we came to a stop at home in under half the time it took to get there.

Chencho leaned over with his hands braced on his knees. "Hooey—you some girl!"

I gulped a few breaths. "And don't you forget it!"

He grinned his cheeky grin and pulled out a ball. We stood kicking it around between the three of us.

Suddenly a boy on an old, rusty bicycle came tearing up. "Belinda—policia—pasaporta!"

The boys quickly told me four policemen with guns had tried to make Belinda get into their police car. She refused and kept saying "No entiendo." (I don't understand.) The little boys told the police she wasn't in charge and the head lady was at home. They were headed for us, and he'd come on ahead to warn us. Chencho ran for Javi and his dad.

When Bel arrived on foot with the police car driving just behind with guns pointed at her, she walked into my arms. "I gotta go home; I gotta go home." Her whisper shot holes into my heart.

"Bel, I'm so, *so* sorry. I should never have left you. I never dreamed anything would happen."

We collected our passports and were tossed into the back of the police car. Javi and his dad came with us. With four of us in the back and the two police in front of the Volkswagen, we were packed in like sardines. The barrel of one guard's machine gun was resting against my head.

"Bel, do machine guns have safety catches on them?" I whispered the question as we went over a series of bumps, and the machine gun thumped a *rat-a-tat-tat* on my forehead.

She yanked me back. "Lean on me; don't let that touch you."

As they stopped in front of the station and we stumbled out of the car, the doors burst open and six guards with machine guns ran out and stationed themselves down the steps.

At the click of the guns sliding bullets in for action, I murmured to Bel, "Boy, I haven't a clue what we did, but it sure must have been big." All the way up the stairs the guns followed our every move.

The chief of police was pretty mad. Thankfully Javi's dad interceded on our behalf, so they didn't lock us behind bars in the dark, cement cells. We were seated on a backless bench in a long, narrow hall. In front of each door at either end a guard with a machine gun pointed toward us stood at tense attention. I don't know how long we spent in jail, but it seemed like an eternity when we had no idea of what we were being accused. Javi simply told us not to say a word, just sit and smile nicely if anyone looked at us.

Eventually we were released. We found out we should have registered with the police when we arrived. Now they thought we were part of the terrorists. The family was accused of negligence in bringing foreigners into their city and told that we should be kept at home and not allowed out alone.

Once we were finally alone in our room, we both went to pieces in our own fashion. Bel worried me. It was like she was in a trance; she just kept saying, "I've got to go home." I'd never felt so helpless. There was no way I could get us to the airport on our own, and the dad just kept saying it was in God's hands. That was true, but I'm afraid my faith wasn't as strong as his!

Finally I took Bel's hands. "Bel, listen to me. The bombing keeps getting closer, but it hasn't touched our street yet. So I'll promise you this. If they bomb our building on this street, I'll get us out of here, even if I have to kidnap the dad."

"Really?" She finally looked at me.

"Really."

"Okay." She turned over and soon was asleep. Meanwhile, I lay in bed thinking.

Boy, Stacy, what a stupid thing to promise. How on earth are you going to kidnap somebody? But I promised. I have to keep my promise. Sheesh. What am I going to do? After a few moments, another thought floated to the front. *Duh, Stacy, if they bomb this building, we're in it. I won't have to worry about kidnapping anyone. We'll be home all right—in our heavenly home.* At that realization, I calmed down and was actually able to sleep as well.

Chapter 18

The next morning we both felt like we might survive after all. However, I definitely needed communication with my family. The one-year anniversary of my brother's death was approaching, and I knew my family was planning to be together at Cheryl's place over that time.

Bel knew how desperate I was feeling and approached Javi.

"Stacy really needs to call her family. Even if it takes all day, we need to go to the phone building."

Javi agreed and walked down with us. Those two patiently waited for two hours with me as we tried and tried and tried to get through. Finally, the operator called me over to take the line.

Through the crackle, hiss, and *ffzzzz* of the phone line, I heard my father's voice.

"Hello, hello? Is anyone there?"

"Dad, it's me! Stacy. I thought I'd never get through—"

"Is anyone on the line? I can't hear you."

I started shouting. "Dad, it's me, Stacy. I've tried for two hours to call." Over the wire I heard my whole family talking about who could be on the line. Mom's voice was faint but clear.

"Art, could it be Stacy? Remember how the only time she got through it was all crackly? Stacy? Are you there? It's me, Mom."

My voice wobbled. "Yes, Mom, I'm here—"

"Oh, dear, I can't hear anything, but who else would have such trouble on the line?"

I could hear them so clearly and yelled madly into the phone, hoping that would somehow help. "It's me; it's me. I can hear you. Please, just keep talking!"

Dad's voice came through again. "Honey, if that's you, be assured that we love you and are praying for you."

I could hear the finality in his voice and cried out. "I can hear you. Please, please don't hang up. It's okay you can't hear me—just talk to me!"

But he continued, to my utter despair. "But I'm going to hang up now."

"No, no!" I screamed into the phone. Click. The line went dead. I stared in stunned silence at the phone receiver. I couldn't believe it. My dad, my rock and mainstay all my life, had just hung up on me in my deepest hour of need. I think at that moment I could understand to an infinitesimal speck why Christ cried out on the cross, "My God, my God, why have you forsaken me?" With tears streaming down my cheeks, I turned and marched out of that building. Bel started up to meet me, but after one look at me and my whispered "leave me be," she sank back into her chair.

I walked outside and stood looking over the bleak, barren landscape. I was in my own Garden of Gethsemane of bitterness and anguish of spirit.

I am going to die in this god-forsaken place. Into the stillness of that moment, I felt God respond.

I am still here, and I am still God.

But God, why couldn't You at least let me talk to my family?

Am I sufficient for you or not?

I want You to be, but this is so hard. I can't do it.

No, you can't. Not without Me.

The bombing rocked us off our beds last night, Lord.

Yea, thou I walk through the valley of the shadow of death, I will fear no evil, for thou art with me ...

As Psalm 23:6 floated through my mind, I felt a resignation seep through me.

Okay, Lord. Whatever You have in mind, help me be willing.

Just keep holding on to Me.

Bel came out of the building and cautiously approached. I tried to manage a grin, but it was pretty shaky. "Sorry. It was just too much having Dad hang up on me; I felt abandoned."

"No problem. You've seen my spells of bawling, too. I never realized how much we take our good life for granted."

"Yeah, when we get home, I think I'll just sit by the phone touching it reverently."

We walked in silence. I broke it to simply say, "However much this is hard and dangerous for you, God knew what He was doing when He sent you with me. I'm so glad you're here with me."

She grinned. "Can't believe I'm saying this, but I am, too. Maybe not glad to be in this, but glad you aren't alone."

One day Javi said his father needed to talk to us.

"It's getting too dangerous for you here. Our city is a red zone right now, so we want to send you away for a week. I have a missionary friend up in the Andes whom I've contacted. He wasn't home at the time, but the woman working in his home said it would be fine for you to spend a week there. Pack up and be ready to go with Javi on the bus tomorrow."

Chapter 19

We had to get up at 4:00 a.m. to catch a bus into Lima to catch the bus headed for Huascaran. We were excited to be heading for the highest mountain in Peru, so we managed to do it without too much hassle. However, the bus ride getting there was not so fun. Even on a nine-hour bus trip they still allow people on when every seat is full, so a lot of the time we were crammed in, with people taking turns standing in the aisles. Of greater concern for me was the bathroom break. There was only one stop on the trip. I didn't think I'd survive. By God's grace I managed to make it until we pulled into the bus stop. Of course, then the lineup to use the toilet was long, but eventually Bel and I got to go into the narrow concrete stalls. I took one look and laughed.

Bel's voice floated over to me. "Where's the toilet?"

"See the small hole in the ground?"

"Yeah."

"That's the toilet."

"What? Then what are the two small bricks on either side of it for?"

"Stand on them. That puts your feet out of range."

"Ooh, so gross."

"Hey, after four and a half hours, I'm just thankful for the privacy of these concrete walls. Another bump on the road and I'd have been in big trouble."

Although I missed out on that trouble, I certainly created a problem in the next few minutes. Wandering back to the bus before Belinda, I spied the edge of her pillow sticking out the window. I grinned. Bel had teased me so much about not having a pillow since I'd given her a hassle about lugging it all the way to Peru, that I decided here was my chance to get her back. I eased over to the window and by standing on tiptoe could just catch the edge of it. I was going to pull it out and then tease her about what I found at this bus stop, and finders' keepers, etc. However, just as I started pulling it, there were shouts and running feet, and the next thing I knew, my body was slammed against the side of the bus. A sharp pain seared through me, but I didn't have time to think about it as I was flipped around and forced back against the bus with a pair of hands wrapped around my throat. Several men were shaking me and yelling something.

As a crowd gathered, Javi and Bel came running. In the midst of a flurry of Spanish, Javi pulled the hands away from my neck. Bel pushed the men away and grabbed my arm.

"Stacy, you're bleeding badly!"

I looked down at my wrist she was trying to pinch together. Blood was spurting out of a jagged tear just below my hand.

"Ah, that was the pain. I guess I sliced it open when they dragged me from the window."

Bel tried to let go and blood spurted again. "Stacy, I think it might have nicked the artery. What are we going to do?"

I was feeling shaky and slid to the ground. "Just keep holding on to it and pray. Oh yeah, and remind me never to play a practical joke again." I stared over at the group of men. "What was that all about?"

Javi turned around. "Theft is a huge problem in Peru. They knew that pillow belonged to the darker white girl, so they thought you were stealing it."

"What were they yelling?"

He grinned. "Ladrona; it means thief, robber, crook."

"All right, all right. I get the picture."

Bel jumped up and marched over to the men. She pointed at me. "Mi amiga, mi amiga." The men were aghast that her friend would consider stealing from her. We left Javi to try to explain it was a personal joke between friends while we tried the best we could to patch me up.

Bel pulled out our alcohol swabs. "I think this might hurt, but we sure don't want it to get infected like your toe did." I let go of the broken skin I was holding shut for a brief moment and she slapped the alcohol swab straight on the open wound. I screamed and the crowd turned to stare at us. A few men stepped toward us.

I gritted my teeth, smiled, and called out, "No problemo. Mi amiga."

They stared at the tears leaking from my eyes despite my best efforts and then at Bel. Turning to Javi, one man made circular motions with a finger at the side of his head. "Tus amigas poco loco."

Bel and I knew we'd just been called a little crazy. We looked at each other as we sat in the dirt with our backs against the bus tire, Belinda holding my arm above my heart to try and slow the bleeding down, and we both laughed. Then they really thought we were crazy.

"Bel, if we make it out of this country alive, you'll forever have a special place in my heart."

"I should have taken a nursing course before coming with you." She fussed with the wound. "Now what do we do?"

We heard a commotion and looked around. A huge argument was going on with the bus driver and some of the people. Javi came over. "There's a problem. They insulted the man, and he's refusing to drive the bus. It may take a while."

I looked at Bel. "There's one good thing to come out of this commotion. At least that'll give us time to fix this."

While the argument continued, we walked over to the gourd that held some brackish water. We hesitated and then poured it over the jagged edges of my skin, slapped more swabs around the wound to my subdued shrieks, and dug in our bags for the cleanest sock to use as padding. Between Bel's help and our fervent prayers, somehow I stopped bleeding. It healed fairly well, and to this day I have just a small scar to remind me to think a joke through before acting on it.

The argument finally ended when the men literally picked up the bus driver, carried him over to the bus, and plopped him in his seat. He sat there with his arms stubbornly folded, but after someone handed him some money, he unfolded his arms and called out, "Vamos, vamos." We scrambled back to our seats, and the bus lurched its way back onto the road half an hour later than we should have been. We'd already learned time meant nothing to these people, so I was only a little annoyed at the delay.

The rest of the trip went fairly well, although we still had to be very careful with my wrist. The winding, narrow roads as we took switchback after switchback made both of us a bit nauseated, but the scenery was incredible. Mt.

Huascaran was the highest mountain in Peru. Thatched-roof huts and men using a donkey to plow a small patch of land in front of the hut were common sights from our window. The view made me think of Psalm 8, where it talks about the majesty of all God has created. But I was glad I didn't live there. We were on our fourth switchback, and when I glanced out the window, I could see the three previous loops we'd just come around below us.

Eventually we pulled into the town nestled somewhere on this mountain. As we pulled into what should have been the bus stop, the entire bus went eerily silent. Instead of the station, there was just rubble. We drew as near as possible, and people got off. We waited until Javi could find out what happened.

The sorrow in his eyes made me forget a bit of my fear. "There was a bomb set off here."

"How long ago?"

"Half an hour. It was set for when the bus should have pulled in. These guerrillas are everywhere. My poor country."

A shiver went through me. If that bus driver hadn't been so stubborn about something and we had been on time, we'd be dead.

God, I'm sorry for my impatience with these people and their sense of time.

Remember that, child, the next time you get angry at the procrastination. Time is important, but sometimes other things are just as important.

Well, I'll think about being late to a bombing, and that should help!

That's why these experiences are good for you. They stretch you to look from someone else's point of view, not just your own.

We gathered our luggage and set off to find the place where we were to stay. It took a long time to get there, as we constantly had to stop.

Bel commented. "I never knew I was such a wimp. I can barely walk, let alone carry my suitcase without puffing."

I plopped my suitcase sideways onto the dirt and sat on it. "You're not a wimp. We're just really high up. My head is aching."

Javi sat on the ground. "Mt. Huascaran is our highest peak. It's over 22,000 feet. This town is close to 16,000 feet, so you're going to be headachy and short of breath for a while. Don't push it too hard or you'll get altitude sickness."

He was right. It took most of the week we were there to finally adjust to the limited oxygen, and by then we were ready to leave.

"These headaches are so weird," I complained to Bel one night in our bed.

"Yeah, I feel like I've got five 'ice cream' headaches all going on at the same time in different parts of my head."

"Good thing we brought a whole bottle of Tylenol along—although I'm not sure how much good they do for this type of headache."

"Don't tell me that; let me at least pretend it's helping!" Bel rolled over and reached for our bottle. "We can't let headaches stop us from exploring." So we didn't.

After finding our "home," Sarita let us in. She only spoke Spanish, but we managed to communicate with her by signs and motions when Javi wasn't available.

"The family went off to another village to preach, so they don't know you're here, but no problem. Just make yourselves at home. They'll be back sometime late tonight." She showed us into our bedroom. As we opened our suitcases, I spied something hanging on the wall. It looked like a huge, over-sized toilet paper roll, but it was cream and brown with stripes running like diamonds along it.

I pointed my finger. "What's that?"

Sarita laughed, went over, and started pulling on it. Out and out across the room it kept unfurling. Javi heard the commotion and came to see what Sarita was saying.

"Oh, that's a boa constrictor skin," he explained. He listened a bit and then his eyes widened and he whistled.

Bel and I stared at him. "Well, go on," Bel snapped. "Don't leave us in suspense."

"The pastor was on his way through the jungle to preach at a village when this dropped out of a tree he was walking under. He got his rifle up in time to shoot her, so he didn't have to be her dinner."

"How do you know it was a 'she?'" Bel lifted an eyebrow. "It could have been a 'he.'"

Javi grinned. "Nah, first off, we men aren't so nasty. Secondly, this is over ten feet long. Most males don't get that big."

I shook my head as I fingered the snake skin. "Well, all I can say is that man must have amazing target skills. I better not get on his bad side!" We laughed, but I didn't realize how prophetic those words would be.

We left our stuff and headed off to explore with Javi—to explore slowly.

I'd never thought about needing to breathe. Normally you just did it. Now, we felt every breath we took.

Javi had a friend, Mateo, in the area, although he'd never been here to visit him. Mateo had some great ideas of things to do. As we wandered through a shop looking at things, a huge sense of disquiet came over me. I didn't hear an audible voice, but there was an inner prompting: *leave this building*. I tried to shake it off, but instead it became more persistent. Finally, I nudged Bel.

"Bel, you're going to think I'm crazy, but I think we need to get out of here."

She paused in the middle of putting a shawl back. "Why?"

"I don't know; something just seems to be telling me to go."

She cocked her head. "Really? Wow. How strong?"

"Strong enough I'm going. If you want to stay, that's fine. I'll wait for you somewhere."

She dropped the stuff. "No way. I'll come. The last time you left me alone, remember what happened!"

"I'm sure I'm being paranoid, but—"

"No, that's fine."

We told Javi we were done here and wanted to leave immediately. He stared at me and then shrugged. "Girls! They can never make up their minds. You're the ones who begged to stop here."

I started briskly away. "Yeah, well, now we're done."

We had walked a good number of blocks when suddenly, *b-o-o-m*! A vibration shook the building we were beside, and a bit of dust drifted down over us. We looked back in the direction we'd just come from and saw a cloud of dust, particles, and what-not in the sky.

Bel's eyes popped, my jaw dropped, and the boys stared at us incredulously.

Javi spoke slowly. "Man, it's a good thing we left when we did, otherwise..." He stared at me and I just shrugged. After a few solemn moments, we continued to walk. Bel sidled up to me.

"Tell me again how you knew we needed to leave."

"I honestly don't know, Bel, except this phenomenal feeling kept nagging me: *leave, get out, go now*. I can't explain it except that God is keeping us alive. It's good we obeyed."

"Well, if you ever get that feeling again, just let me know. If God is prompting you on where we should be to stay safe, let's not ignore Him!"

As we walked, I sent a prayer upward.
Thanks, God. And thank you for not letting up on me until I obeyed.
You're welcome, My child.

We went to a fancy restaurant where they had a male quartet playing panpipes and unique Peruvian instruments. It was a great time. Upon our return home, there were a few deaf girls at the house. I was amazed that I could understand enough signs to catch the gist of what they were saying. It'd been eight years since I'd learned some sign language. Javi translated Spanish to English for us, and I translated the deaf girls' sign language into English for Javi so he could tell Mateo and Sarita in Spanish what the girls were saying. Thus we managed to have a lovely evening of fun and games despite the language barriers.

That night, Bel became violently ill. I wasn't sure if it was food poisoning. She had tried some exotic food at the restaurant. First the shakes were so bad she vibrated the bed. Then I realized she felt like a block of ice.

She moaned. "I'm so sick; I'm so sorry."

I hushed her. "Bel, stop that. It's not your fault. How many times have you had to hold the bucket for me and clean up because of my sensitive stomach. This is just turn around, fair play." I didn't want her to know how worried I was. Some of the stuff she spouted to me was just gibberish. I finally lay on top of her to try to warm her up as well as hold her on the bed. My prayers were absolute pleadings.

God, please, I don't know what's wrong with her. I don't know what to do.
Keep praying.
This is beyond sick, Lord. This is deathly. Please don't let her die.
Keep praying.
If anyone has to die, let it be me. I can't go home alone and face her parents.
Keep praying.

I started to quote every Bible verse I could think of about prayer and faith. Around 3:00 a.m., she gave me a violent shove. "Move. I need more than the bucket."

As she stumbled down the hallway, I decided I'd better follow along and clean up any mess. If we slept in, I didn't want someone else to deal with it. The power was off, and I didn't know where Sarita had left the candles, so I used my lighter to flicker a bit of light and glanced along the floor. With a rag in my hand, and the lighter to occasionally recheck my route, I was halfway down the hallway on my hands and knees when I heard a door click open and a voice call out. My thoughts flashed a few messages to my brain, and I caught my breath.

Ooh boy, Stacy. Now you're in for it. Number one—that's the pastor home from his preaching. Number two—he doesn't know he has guests in his house. Number three—he shot a boa constrictor dropping out of a tree. Number four—don't move, don't breathe, and don't stare in his direction. My joking remark about not getting on his bad side came back with a vengeance.

I drew into myself as far as I was able and huddled on the floor with my back against the wall, thanking the Lord the lights weren't working. I heard the man fumble around in his room and then come into the hallway. The *chkk-chkk* of a bullet being inserted into its chamber sounded deadly loud in the blackness of the night. The man passed by within inches of me. I could have reached out and grabbed his ankle.

Stacy, don't even think about doing that. It'd be the last thing you ever did. My fear had a level of hysteria in it.

As he opened the outer door to peer out, I talked to God once more. *God, you know we had permission to be here. Please don't let him shoot me. He'd feel terrible about it—and I wouldn't feel so great, either.*

Another thought struck.

Lord, don't let Bel come out of the bathroom right now, either.

It felt like an eternity before he shut and locked his doors and re-entered his bedroom.

Thanks, Lord!

As soon as I heard snoring, I finished getting down to Bel and checking on her. She was wrung out but not an ice block anymore. I left her there and returned to bed to continue praying. About an hour later, she staggered back to our room. By morning she looked exhausted but alive.

She gazed at me. "That was awful. First, I was scared I was going to die; then I was scared I wouldn't."

I heaved a sigh. "Believe me, I was praying all night that you wouldn't die. I'd rather die if that makes you get home safely."

"Well, I've been praying the same about you, too."

Bel stayed in bed while I went to breakfast and was introduced to the family. They seemed really nice and were more than happy to host us. They knew some broken English.

The pastor shook my hand. "Glad to see you! Glad you here safely. Also, glad I not shoot you. I heard noise last night. We have many thieves around here, and I not know we have guests. I took my gun to go bang, bang! Good thing you were in the bedroom. Ha-ha!"

I smiled weakly. *If only you knew!* "Yeah, good thing. Ha-ha."

Chapter 20

Bel soon bounced back to normal health, and we continued to explore. Each trip was different. We caught a ride however it came: sometimes by bus, once in a tour van, sometimes on the back of somebody's pickup, once in a cattle truck. We just pushed the pigs aside when they got too close. One trip we went to Yungay. In May 1970, an earthquake demolished it as well as another little village. Twenty thousand people died instantly, as they had no time to get out of there. It was considered the largest national disaster of the twentieth century at that time. A memorial to honour the many lost lives was built on the original place, and a new Yungay started a short distance away. It was both special and solemn to walk across that burial ground. I stumbled a fair bit, and when I'd check why, I'd see someone's chimney or the edge of an upturned vehicle sticking out of the ground.

Javi's favourite day was our guided tour higher up the mountain. We were already at sixteen thousand feet, but we could drive another two thousand feet higher and get into the snowline. Javi had never seen snow, so he really wanted to go. Bel and I couldn't have cared less about the snow, but we went along, too. We were warned we'd have to hike up the last way, and to be very careful not to run. Most tourists rented these cute little burros to ride up, but Javi didn't think that was manly. So we walked—and stopped—and puffed. When Javi saw the snow, he broke into a run. He'd only gone a few yards when—*poof*—he went face-flat on the ground. My heart nearly stopped.

"Javi! Don't die! We can't get out of here without you!" I felt selfish when Bel stared at me.

We bent over him and soon saw him start to stir. Bel slapped his back. "Don't you listen? They said, 'Don't run; the air is too thin.' You scared us half to death!" We helped him get up, and when he could breathe properly he walked more circumspectly.

The "snow" wasn't snow by our standards. It was crystalized ice shards. But Javi was ecstatic. He kept feeling it, rubbing it along his face, making balls, and watching it slowly drip from his fingers. We thoroughly enjoyed watching Javi experience snow for the first time.

On the way back down, we had such weird headaches that we rented burros. Javi still insisted on walking, but Bel and I were happy to sit on the burros and let them do all the work.

Even though we were having fun, the tension still was high. One day as we sat eating in a sidewalk cafe, I got extremely antsy as that familiar nagging feeling came over me. As I debated what to do, Bel looked at me.

"You're getting that feeling again, aren't you?"

"Yeah, I am. I was trying to decide how to tell you."

Javi looked at us. "Tell us what?"

"That we need to get out of here."

He stared hard at me. "How do you know that?"

I looked him in the eyes. "I'm not involved. I just have something inside me telling me to move."

Bel looked at him. "God uses many different ways and people to get His message across. Stacy has been given a feeling. That's good enough for me. We're going. Are you coming?"

"I haven't finished my meal." He grumbled as he stood and crammed the last roll into his mouth. "But whatever."

That evening the pastor shared some sad news. "We've had some bombings hit our city again, so be careful when you go out. You're lucky you weren't at that restaurant you mentioned going to. It's not there anymore. That block was bombed this afternoon." When we asked what time it had happened, we found out it was about twenty minutes after we'd left. Javi shot a puzzled frown my way. I didn't know how to reassure him, but I did know Who to thank for bringing us out of there in a timely manner.

One drive we took was nearly a disaster for me in my ignorance. We were winding our way high into the Andes and stopped for a break. There were ten little beggar children standing along the road. We knew we couldn't help everyone, as the poverty was everywhere, but it sure hurt to see the hungry kids when we had so much.

These children were holding bags to sell. They caught my eye because it was the closest thing to a Ziplock bag we'd seen since arriving in Peru. I walked over and saw they had big bunches of leaves inside each bag.

"Brilliant!" I exclaimed as a thought rushed through my brain.

Bel cocked her head. "What's brilliant?"

"My idea."

"A-n-n-d?"

"I need to take souvenirs home for people. What better thing than to bring back real Peruvian tea for my friends? It's light and easy to pack, is authentic, and it'll help these kids."

I pulled out my money and motioned to the children. They rushed to me, pushing each other in their eagerness to be the one to get my business.

"Alto! (stop) No problemo. Uno, uno, uno." I pointed to each child and used my teacher voice. They finally realized I intended to buy a bag from each of them and settled down. As we left, they waved happily to me, while I felt like crying. I'd paid only ten cents a bag. For one dollar, I'd made ten children beam like a sunrise.

I opened my bags and started sniffing. Bel leaned over.

"So what kind have you got?"

"I don't know—definitely not peppermint or lemon. It seems to be a bit flowery, but it's nothing I've smelled before. So I guess I really did get a true Peruvian flavour." I nudged Javi, who hadn't been paying much attention to us as he visited with his friend. "Hey, what kind of tea did I actually buy?"

Javi turned his head and his eyebrows shot up at the fistfuls of leaves I was sniffing.

"You bought all that?"

"Yep. One from each kid."

He frowned. "You like it that much?"

"Oh yeah. I drink it all the time."

Now his eyes also popped. "Really? It doesn't affect you?"

"It makes me feel good—especially in our cold winters."

He nodded slowly. "Guess that's why some call it happy tea."

I frowned. "Happy tea? That's a weird name."

"It does weird things, too. That's why Dad doesn't let us drink it."

Bel and I looked at each other. "You drink tea. We've had it at your place."

"Not this kind."

After digging a bit more, Javi finally told us the name of this "tea" I'd bought.

Bel fell into a laughing fit at my stunned face. "I don't believe it. My teacher just bought ten bags of cocaine!"

"Stop laughing! This isn't funny." I was horrified.

Javi was puzzled at our reaction. "What's wrong?"

Bel cackled. "My teacher just bought thousands of dollars' worth of cocaine for gifts to our church people."

Javi's jaw dropped. "Your country would pay that much for that?" He pointed at my ten cent bags and grinned. "Maybe we should start a business."

"No!" Bel and I shouted simultaneously. "It's totally illegal in our country."

He shrugged. "We're not supposed to have it here either, but it grows so easily up here, you can just pick it. It's also brewed as a tea for altitude sickness and does really help." With that comment stuck in my mind, for the rest of the visit I really hesitated to drink any tea.

It took me a while to dispose of the cocaine. I didn't want to just dump it all where someone might get their hands on it, so I periodically threw a bit out the window. At rest stops, I stuffed some in sewers and tossed some in rivers. Every time Bel saw me toss a handful, she started laughing. I eventually managed to get rid of the last of it, but I kept the bags. Since bags were a hard-to-come-by commodity, I felt like I'd still gotten my ten cents' worth and kept them to use.

One evening the four of us went to a special hotel for a nice meal. It was fun and enjoyable, but just before dessert that sense of "need to leave" came over me. I pushed my plate back and looked at Bel. She caught on.

"You've got 'the feeling' again, don't you?"

"Yep."

Bel turned to Javi. "Let's go."

"We haven't had dessert."

I stood, and Bel joined me. "This was great, but I'm not hungry anymore."

The boys muttered in Spanish but joined us and we left. Half an hour later, a Spanish man spied our white skin and rushed over. He was so excited to see us because he wanted to practise his little knowledge of English.

As he asked where we were staying, Javi mentioned eating at the hotel.

"Aiyee! For when you eat there?" He became agitated.

"Half an hour ago. Why?" I asked.

He made wild motions with his hands. "Hotel, twenty minutes ago—*boom*! You lucky!" He made the sign of the cross.

Javi turned and looked at me with awe and fear alternating across his face. "How do you know?"

The man stepped toward me, and in that moment with the inky, cool darkness surrounding us, a fiery light slashed in front of my eyes, almost blinding me. As I shielded my eyes, I saw the forms of four angels. Their backs were to me, and from wingtip to wingtip they held our little group inside their brilliance and kept the Spanish people outside the circle.

I gulped. My voice quavered. "Bel?"

"What?" She sounded normal.

"Do you see them?" They were so bright I could barely squint at them.

"See what?" Bel looked at my shaking hands. "What's wrong?"

"You don't see any angels?"

"Stacy, what's going on?"

I blinked and rubbed my eyes, but they were still there. They held flaming swords in their hands. The shimmering light in the deepest centre was so bright it was blue and then fanned outward into a yellowish-white flame edged in crimson. As that man stepped toward me, two angels lowered their swords so they crossed in a "v" with the man's head in the centre.

In the midst of my stupification and awe, Philippians 4:7 flashed through my mind: "And the peace of God, which passeth all understanding, shall keep your hearts and minds through Christ Jesus." As I saw the swords descending to stop the man from touching me, a wave of such peace rolled over me, it almost knocked me off my feet. I turned to Bel.

"Bel—we're going to be okay. There's no way anyone can kill us unless God allows it." In awe I stretched my shaking hand out toward the apparitions, and—*poof*—they disappeared. I was left in inky blackness. Once again, I was blinded by the extreme light-to-darkness switch over.

Bel took my hand. "I don't know what you saw, but please, don't lose it on me. I can't take it down here if something happens to you."

I simply stated again. "Bel, we're going to be okay."

I don't know why God allowed me to glimpse that when Bel didn't get to see it. As the initiator of this trip and her teacher, I felt so much stress and helplessness to keep Bel safe that just as God allowed Elisha's servant in 2 Kings 6:8–17 a glimpse of the invisible help waiting for Israel, so He allowed me that moment's peek into the other-life to give me the peace I needed to finish our time in Peru.

My serenity was so complete after that incident, I occasionally worried Bel.

One day we walked around a corner and saw several bombed buildings that were still smoking. I was too busy looking to notice the soldier until he shoved his machine gun into my stomach and shouted at me. I looked down and imagined the bullet flying out of the gun, buzzing around my body, and diving back down into the barrel. It made me laugh. The shocked look on his face as I patted the gun and said, "bueno; bueno," made me feel sorry for him. I patted his arm and tried again. "No problemo. Esta beuno." Bel came running over to drag me away from him.

"You're cracking up on me, Stacy. Come on, don't lose it."

"I'm truly okay. Don't worry."

In spite of the troubles that had seemed to follow us, we'd had a good time high up in the magnificent Andes Mountains. When the day came to say goodbye to our hosts, we were sad to step onto the bus for the long ride back to Javi's home. But when we finally arrived, dusty and disheveled, it was good to be back with his family again.

Chapter 21

By the time we were back, things seemed to have settled down a bit in our own city, or else we were becoming inured to everything. But we still never knew what each day would bring. So many close calls reminded us of our mortality. I knew beyond a shadow of a doubt that God had His hand over us, but I also knew that our timing is not always His timing. So when we were in Lima one day and saw some street artists at work, I turned to Bel.

"Say, why don't we get a couple of these guys to draw us? If we don't make it out of here, Javi could send these papers to our families."

"That's a great idea—except for the end part," Bel quickly nodded.

I frowned. "The end part?"

Bel slapped my back. "Yeah, no sense in Javi sending the papers through the mail. I think it's a much better idea to just take them home and give them to our families ourselves!"

"Right!"

We found two men eager for our five dollars. So we sat together on a bench, and each man quickly did a charcoal drawing of our faces. I was impressed with how good they were and how quickly they finished.

Our time of departure was getting closer, so Javi dropped our Spanish lessons and had us focus more and longer time periods with each of the classes. Bel really enjoyed working with the little ones, while I liked the challenge of the older students. However, they stretched my patience many times, as I'm extremely time-oriented and they were anything but!

I'd assigned Javi an English essay and waited and waited for it. I was giving him a lot of leeway, as he was gone much of the time. He still attended classes in university a couple of days a week and spent so much time helping us. But I came to the end of my patience one day.

"Javi, that essay is several weeks overdue. I'm not giving you another lesson until you hand in the essay." I prepared myself for a round of excuses, but to my astonishment, he simply reached into his bag, shuffled a few things, pulled out the completed essay, and handed it to me.

I quickly glanced at it and shot a quizzical look at him. "This looks great. How long ago did you finish it?"

"A week or so."

Placing my hands on my hips I glared at him. "So why didn't you hand it in?"

He shrugged. "You never asked for it."

Another time, I was nagging Diego. He had a good grasp of English but tried to do as little as possible. "Diego, there's no reason this shouldn't be done. You sat around doing nothing all evening."

"But that is so fun."

"Sitting around doing nothing is fun?"

"Much more fun than sitting around working on an essay!"

I gave him a scolding, but Diego just grinned.

I huffed a breath of exasperation. "What's so funny now?"

"You. You should be a preacher. You're great at giving sermons."

"Very funny. I would not be a preacher."

He paused and thought a moment. "Okay. You should be a preacher's wife."

"What? Why?"

"You could write all his sermons for him."

Although we were dependent on Javi and his family for so much and needed to be careful about leaving the compound, occasionally our Canadian independence would flare and we'd throw a mild rebellion. On one such instance, Bel and I left the school in the afternoon to go for a walk. The boys were busy and couldn't go, and we didn't want to wait. It was just one of those days when we had to get away and have a bit of freedom. So we slipped out of the house without telling anyone we were going.

"Wow! An adventure—we've slipped the leash. What are we going to do?" I rounded the corner with Bel.

"I'm dying for a sandwich. Let's go to the marketplace and see if we can find something."

I nodded agreement and we stepped along quickly. "When we get back to Canada, I'm going to spend the first hour walking in and out of the house."

Bel's face twitched. "Ah yes, the freedom to walk wherever and whenever we want and for how long we want. I think it'll be a while before I take that for granted again."

We made it to the marketplace and even found something that resembled a hamburger. After buying it, we turned around and spied a trail of children following us.

"Ok, Bel, now what?" I mumbled through a mouthful of food.

"Let's lose them; we don't want to spend our free time being pinched and poked and jabbered to."

We quickly started winding our way between booths and ducking into alleys. I finally stopped for breath.

"We did it. We lost them ... only I think we lost ourselves, too! Do you have any idea where we are?"

"No, but let's try to track our way back. If we get back to the hamburger booth, I know how to get us home." Bel set her jaw and turned to enter the maze we'd just left. I have no sense of direction whatsoever. I can get lost on a straight mile, so that meant I just trailed along behind Bel. We spent forty-five minutes wandering the streets. Because the power was off, we became increasingly anxious to get home. Even though we'd had this moment of rebellion, we knew two white girls alone on the streets after dark was a bad scenario. The other thing that made it difficult was that the vendors were packing up and leaving, so the landmarks Bel had used to pinpoint our location had disappeared.

As we fumbled through an alley and made a turn, I ran into a policeman.

"Hola." He started to speak, and then his eyes widened and he rattled off a cannonade of Spanish that we didn't have a clue how to interpret. He pointed his finger at us. "Vamos! Vamos." Soon we were marching in front of him at a rapid pace.

"Ooh boy, Bel. I'm not sure what's going to happen, but this is not looking good."

Bel had a thoughtful look on her face. "Actually, this might not be bad."

I tried to stare at her while being pushed forward in such a manner. "How's that?"

She twisted her head to look at the man. "I think this is the same guy who was at the police station when we were hauled in the first time."

She was right. To our embarrassment, he marched us all the way home. Once we were back in the right area and Bel knew where we were, we did our best to convince him to just let us go. But he wouldn't.

When Javi opened the door, the policeman let out a barrage of Spanish. Soon the dad, mom, and Javi were in an intense conversation with him.

I whispered out of the corner of my mouth. "Ouch. I feel like a recalcitrant schoolkid being hauled in for playing hooky." Bel snorted but then quickly assumed a solemn expression when the policeman turned and glared at us.

When he finally left, we found out Bel was right. He was one of the ones who had warned the family not to let us out alone because it was too dangerous. I felt terrible that we'd caused the family problems, but sometimes we felt so cloistered that it was hard to be obedient.

As the countdown towards September 12 crept closer, the family went out of their way to give us some wonderful memories to take back. They took us to a Peruvian folk music festival and out to a special restaurant whenever it was safe to do so. I was humbled by their efforts to give us good memories in the midst of the turmoil their country was in. I don't know if I'd have the fortitude to look after a couple of foreigners so well if my country was in a state of war. It made me take a good look at myself and realize I had a lot of character-building yet to do in my life.

The youth group had a bonfire night. It was the first time I'd experienced a "progressive bonfire." There was a massive pile of wood in the middle of the yard that had four strings running out of the centre pile for several yards, like a cross. They poured gasoline along the strings and on the wood. Everyone sat on benches around the bonfire with guitars and other Peruvian-made instruments. At exactly the same moment, a boy at each corner of the cross dropped a match on the string. With a *whoosh*, four lines of fire headed toward the centre mass. The others started singing, but I was too entranced watching the fiery cross. Suddenly there was a *boom*, and the centre exploded into a fiery mass. I turned to Belinda.

"Wow! Now we know how to start our campfires in the Rockies!"

She laughed. "That was totally cool. But somehow I don't think it would go over so well in Canada."

Everyone wanted to host us one last time before we left, so the last two weeks were our busiest social ones. If the power was on, we'd play games at places. If it was off, then the candles came out and we'd sit and sing. Bel and I did many duets for people and at services, Diego had me give a flute/piano duet with him for the last Sunday service, and whenever the power was on, we'd use the tape player to record some of our English songs for them to listen to after we were gone.

It was a bittersweet time. On one hand we were so ready to get back to our own country, but the knowledge that this was the last time we'd see these people pulled on our heartstrings. It's astonishing how the frustrations and fears melt away when the reality of never having it again hits. You remember the good times instead of the bad. Of course, I became a basket-case when we had to say goodbye. Watching people waving and holding their handkerchiefs, with tears running down many cheeks, rips me up inside. As a result, it's something I try to get through and over as quickly as possible.

Eventually the last goodbye was said, and we rode away with Javi and his dad for the last journey to Lima and to the airport. Once again, we had to have the last goodbye.

Javi gave me a hug. "Thanks for letting me be your brother. You have been so good for me. I never had a big sister before."

I tried my best not to cry. "Javi, we'd never have survived without you. Thank you so much for putting up with us constantly being around."

Bel added her voice. "If you ever get to Canada, you have a place with us."

As we walked through the turnstile to customs, we were both sniffling. Once we'd made it through the maze of customs and reached our boarding gate, we turned to each other.

"Home! We're going home, Bel. I can't believe it." She reached out and pinched my arm. "Hey! Buzz off. I had enough of that these past three months. Don't you start it now, too."

She laughed. "Just proving to you that you're real; we're alive and about to board a plane—home!" Our eyes started to glisten again, but for a totally different reason.

Chapter 22

The long flight home gave us plenty of time to chat about what might be different and what was the first thing we wanted to do and see. For both of us a long, hot bubble bath was a top priority. We even played rock, paper, and scissors to see who'd get to use the tub first.

When we landed in Los Angeles and walked into the airport, I blinked. The place was dazzling.

"Bel, do you remember when we arrived in LA three months ago. You didn't want to let the suitcase sit on the floor because it was so dirty. Now my eyes hurt it sparkles so much."

Her head bobbed in agreement. "I wouldn't hesitate to pick a hamburger off the floor now and eat it, it seems so clean."

"I think we're both going to have to remember that even though we're home, there's a thing called 'reverse culture shock' that we'll probably experience. It'll take a bit of time to get used to everything here again. These three months have changed us."

Since Belinda had flown on a Canadian passport, while I had an American one, we had to go through customs at different places. We agreed to meet again just outside customs, and then we headed to our separate lines.

As I stood around waiting, I saw a tall man with dark shades and a dog coming toward me. To my amazement, the dog came right at me. I quickly shuffled my suitcases away and to the side, but the dog followed. Once again I tried to move out of the way, but the dog veered at me. Then to my horror, the man pulled a gun out of his holster and pointed it at me.

Lord! I don't believe this. I've spent three months in a foreign country having guns pulled on me, and now I'm not in my own country half an hour and a man does it here?

Listen to the man, Stacy.

Oh, yeah, right. I looked at the man. He motioned me away from the suitcases with the end of his gun.

"Move aside and let the dog check the bags." As I watched the dog circle my bags sniffing, a lightbulb suddenly went on in my brain.

My eyes lit up and my mouth opened before my brain engaged fully. "Oh! I get it. That's a sniffer dog!"

The man pulled his shades off and stared at me. "What else would he be?"

I shrugged and looked sheepishly at him. "I thought you were blind." His eyebrows shot skyward and I defended myself. "Hey, I have friends that are blind, and you were wearing shades inside an airport and had a dog. I felt sorry for you to be alone in an airport with such an untrained dog. I thought I'd help by making sure I was out of your way."

He laughed and put his gun away. "To the contrary, he is a very highly trained dog. You've just come out of Peru, which was in the midst of guerrilla warfare. Drugs are a huge contributor to accessing money for weapons and ammo, so we have to check that people aren't smuggling drugs into our country. Now I know a sweet young thing like you would never do such a thing, but we have to do our job."

I think he droned on some more, but as soon as he mentioned smuggling drugs, my mind flashed back to the bags and bags of cocaine I'd accidentally bought. Some of my stuff inside the suitcase was wrapped in those bags that I'd kept. My heart started racing, my legs quivered, and I broke out in a cold sweat.

Please, Lord, don't let that dog smell any cocaine residue from those bags. You know I did throw it all away.

The man looked at me. "Are you okay? I know it's hard waiting after such a long flight. We'll soon be done. I'm sure you wouldn't ever touch any of this nasty stuff."

I smiled weakly. *Please, Lord, don't let that dog sit. How would I explain I'm dumb enough to buy it as gifts for friends, thinking it was just tea.* "No, sir, I don't want to be involved in that kind of stuff." My relief when the dog finished padding around my bags and came back to his handler almost made me light-headed.

He put his hand on my arm. "You need to get something to eat. You look wiped. Shall I go with you?"

"That's so kind of you, but I have a friend waiting for me." *Plus, I don't want to spend any more time close to your dog, in case he changes his mind!* "We came on the same flight but were in different lines."

"All right—and by the way, welcome home!" He gave me a quick salute and then turned and headed away.

"Hey, are you okay?" The voice beside my shoulder caused me to leap a foot in the air. When I landed, I saw Bel's puzzled face. "What has you looking like you've seen a ghost?"

When I told her what happened, she laughed and laughed. I got irritated.

"I don't see what's so funny about it. I could be sitting in jail right now had enough residue been on those bags."

"Well, at least in this one, people would understand English somewhat better than at our last jail episode." She punched my arm. "You and your imagination. You threw out the cocaine, you didn't smuggle it, so what's there to worry about?"

I inhaled slowly and deeply. "Right. Okay. Let's go." As we trundled our suitcases along to the proper conveyor belt to send them on to our next flight, my faintness dissipated. "Well, I learned one thing. I might like to read stories about mysteries and the smugglers in the American Revolution, but boy, I don't think I'd make a good spy or smuggler."

"I agree. You can look guilty even when you're totally innocent."

"Tell me about it. I often got in trouble when my brother did something because he could look so innocent and I never did."

Once our bags were riding the belt on their way to the loading dock, we high-fived each other.

"We're halfway home, Stacy!"

When we finally arrived in Edmonton, Belinda's family was there to greet us. Chaotic greetings created a hubbub mixed with tears and laughter. It felt surreal, like I was in a dream. That feeling expanded as we reached their home, and April told me to call my family immediately. I looked at the phone, at her, and back at the phone.

"What's wrong, Stacy?" She frowned at the look on my face.

"I'm almost not sure I know how to anymore," I whispered as I ran my hand over the phone. I lifted it up, listened to a dial tone, and placed it down again. I almost started to cry. Bel came over to me and put the phone in my hand.

"You can do this, Stacy. You brought me back alive to my family. Now you need to let your family know you're safe, too." We exchanged a look, a look that we'd share many times over the next few months as we adjusted back to a "normal" life that everyone took for granted, but we couldn't. Not after what we'd gone through.

After three months without a phone, my fingers fumbled trying to dial my parents' number. My emotions overwhelmed me when Mom answered.

"Hello."

Silence. I couldn't talk.

"Hello ... hello, is anyone there?"

Finally I whispered into the phone. "Mom, it's me, Stacy."

"Oh dear God, you've brought my daughter back!" Mom's voice trembled, and I knew she was crying.

After a few "thank you, Jesus" murmurs, she called out to Jocelyn. "Go get your father. Stacy's on the line. She's back in Canada." She peppered me with questions, but exhaustion swept over me and I heard everything in a fog. By the time Dad got on the line, I was monosyllabic.

"Stacy, honey, are you in Mayerthorpe?"

"Yes."

"You got out of Peru just fine then."

"Yes."

"We're so thankful to have you safely home again."

"Yes."

"Stacy, you sound tired."

"Yes."

Dad laughed. "You go and get some sleep. We'll call tomorrow night when you're able to function a bit better." My dad knew me well. I go, go, go at 110%, but when I stop, it's a complete dead stop, and I can't function until I have time and space to decompress.

Mrs. Brown had gone all out to celebrate our return. She'd had her own demons to deal with having her youngest daughter incommunicado and in danger. I don't think the prodigal son's father did a better "fatted calf" for his son's return in Luke 15:11–24 than she did for us. The chandelier sparkled over the long oak table spread with her Old Country Rose Royal Albert china dishes. Crystal goblets stood in stately attendance and Battenberg lace serviettes lay beneath the elegant silverware. The contrast between what lay in front of me and what I'd just left behind gave me sensory overload. I felt shell-shocked the entire time I was enjoying her roast beef with new potatoes, peas, fresh tomatoes, and cucumber slices. The scrumptious cheesecake was the last item I was to enjoy for several hours.

Because my rental house was no longer available, the Browns had agreed to have me board with them for the school year. Soon after we finished eating, I retired to my room. I felt befuddled, confused, and nauseated. I didn't realize that after three months of stomach issues from spicy food, eating a full-fledged, home-cooked meal was not a good idea. Shortly after I heard everyone go to bed, I crept to the bathroom and spent the next several hours resting with my head against the stool. I didn't have the strength to move too far away. I sobbed as quietly as I could.

Lord, you got me home, but now what? I'm just as sick as I was down there. Am I ever going to be normal again? Lord, I'm home, but this hurts. Everything is so bright, so busy, so ... Lord, this isn't how it was supposed to be!

My child, I'm still with you. In the good and in the bad.

But I left the bad behind. I'm supposed to be in the good now, and it feels bad. Help!

It will take time, My child. Take one day at a time.

Can't I turn the clock ahead?

No.

Rats.

I was with you down there. I am with you here.

When my stomach had completely emptied, I crawled back to bed. After a few hours I realized my next problem. Neither Belinda nor I had ever shared a room before Peru, but down there, we didn't have a choice. We slept back-to-back, both for warmth and for protection.

After three months of that, to suddenly have a whole bed to myself felt horrible and scary. I felt like a part of me was missing. My empathy blossomed as I realized this must be how widows feel when their husbands die. I'd only experienced this for three months. How much worse it would be after decades of marriage.

I tossed and turned a few hours. The urge increased.

Stacy, don't you dare go down to Belinda's bedroom. She'd think you were crazy. She's finally got her own bed and would be disgusted if you told her you were scared to sleep alone. How dumb is that? You're in Canada, safely home. Nothing is going to happen to you.

No matter how I reasoned, I couldn't feel safe enough to fall asleep. Suddenly at 4:00 a.m., my door burst open and Bel charged in carrying her pillow.

"I don't care if you think I'm crazy; I can't sleep down there alone. Shove over." I gladly moved over, and we quickly moved into our back-to-back position once again. Within minutes Bel was sleeping, and I soon followed. Mrs. Brown found us like that hours later when she popped her head into my room to see if I knew where Bel had gone. It took us about a week to feel safe enough to sleep alone. Sudden door slams would sometimes send me to the floor.

Later April talked to me alone. "I can't begin to imagine what you girls must have gone through. In fact, I'm not sure I even want to know. But I thought this might help you." She handed me the *Edmonton Journal*. The headlines read: "Police Capture Shining Path Guerrilla Chief." Tears shimmered in her eyes. "Look at the date." I checked. It was the same day we had boarded our plane in Lima. "God certainly had His hand of protection on you girls. It says here in the past decade over 25,000 have died because of this man. I shall forever be grateful to Javi's mom and dad for keeping you safe down there."

Although I was rock-solid certain we'd had angelic intervention during our stay there, I was still human. The fact that we were safely home may have brought me out of the "survival mode" I'd been living in for the past few months. Whatever the reason, once I read that newspaper article and knew the man had actually been captured and was behind bars, I became victim to horrific nightmares. It puzzled me that I'd never suffered nightmares down in Peru when I'd been scared for my life. Yet now that I was safely home, I was plagued by them. I guess my nervous system decided to take a break. Many nights I dreamed the soldiers were after me on one side and the guerrillas were coming at me from the other way. I'd grab for Belinda to drag her down and throw myself on top of her just as a bullet struck me. I'd awaken on the floor with my heart pounding almost out of my body, covered in sweat, and holding on to the pillow for dear life. Another time I would be trying to run from a bomb. The explosion ripped into me, awakening me, and I'd find my sheets were totally entangled around me. They were so saturated with sweat, they dripped.

I was mortified that sometimes my screams would wake the entire family. It took a good three months for the nightmares to die down to occasional episodes. Later on, Dad told me it was over three years before they felt like they saw their real Stacy emerge. I was much more cautious. When entering a building, I'd immediately check for a second exit. There was no more sitting in the middle of a pew at church. I needed to sit at the end of a row, toward the back, and close to an exit. It sure made me wonder how soldiers ever readjusted after a tour of duty.

In the transition back home, there were also things that were just funny. Our first Sunday in church, I stood at the door and my mouth dropped.

Bel nudged me. "Move on. What's holding you up?"

I kept staring. "Did they institute a new church law while we were gone?"

She looked puzzled. "It all looks the same. What are you talking about?"

"Do they allow only blondes into this church? Everyone is so white and light. Did they all dye their hair while we were gone?"

Bel laughed. "You are so weird; of course not. But it's been three months since we've seen anyone with white skin, let alone blonde hair, so yeah, it's kinda strange."

What Bel said struck me. "Oh wow, if it feels this weird in just three months, no wonder we were such a shock to the Peruvians, who'd never seen white skin like ours. I shouldn't have been so annoyed at their constant pinching to see if it was real."

"If it makes you feel better, I can pinch you once a day."

"No, thanks for your generosity, but I'll pass."

Bel committed the next faux pas. She pointed at the piano. "Hey, do you think Bert has gained weight since we left?" Bert turned and stared at her while I poked her in the ribs.

"Bel, everyone can understand us now. In Peru, we could point at one thing while we discussed a person right under his nose. They just assumed we were talking about what we pointed at. I think Bert heard you."

"Oops." She giggled.

Belinda had graduated that spring, so she was free to do whatever she wanted as she adjusted back to Canada. However, school had already been going a week, so I was back in the classroom the day after we arrived. Since I'd had everything prepared before I left, knowing I'd be late coming back, everything was running smoothly. This was good, as the reverse culture shock was harder than I'd expected. I'm not sure what the students felt about the changes in their teacher.

Molly came in one day to see me turning the light switch on, then off, then on, then ...

"Miss K, is something wrong?"

"No. Why?"

"Why do you keep flipping the light switch?"

"Because I can." I left the switch and moved over to my desk, leaving her staring after me.

Another day it was Faith who came into the washroom as I flushed the toilet several times.

"Miss K, what are you doing now?"

"Watching the water. Do you realize I didn't carry a single drop of that water? It disappears and reappears. How wonderful is that, hmm?"

Very slowly I made my way back into a world where one takes things for granted. I don't regret having gone through some of that tough stuff, though. I don't think I will ever forget what it's like to be without; I appreciate what I do have now and don't take it for granted as easily. Mind you, I still had my moments of struggle with God.

God, how can this be so hard? I might just as well have stayed in Peru.

Do you really want to be back there?

Well, no, but all these nightmares and the jumpiness is terrible. Down there I never had this.

You were in survival mode. Now you have to decompress.

Can't you just take it all away?

In your weakness, you remember to depend on Me. In your strength, it's easy to forget.

What if I promise to remember?

If everything were easy in life, how would you learn to have compassion for others who are struggling?

Grrr, I guess you're right, but that doesn't mean I like this!
Growth can be painful, but you will come out stronger.

I don't know if part of the reason the return was so hard on me was that now that I wasn't focused on staying alive, grief for the death of my brother also surfaced again. We had entered the second year without him, and that pain doesn't just disappear.

One day my sister-in-law, Cheryl, contacted me.

"Stacy, I'm about to go crazy here at home without Nick. I need to get away for a bit."

"Where are you going?"

"Well, I wondered if you wanted to take a trip with me. You love travelling, and perhaps with your stresses right now, you might want to get away, too."

"Oh, wow. Yeah, but how, when, where?"

"Don't you have spring break and Easter break? Could you get away then? As for where, I'd like to go east. I know you've wanted to go to Newfoundland, so maybe we could head that way."

My ears perked up. "Oh, man, yeah. That would be great. Let me work around this end and see what I can make work."

When I checked the calendar and schedules, I decided that this would be doable, and it might just help me get past some of my stresses from Peru. I'd never heard of PTSD, but in retrospect, I think I had a fairly severe case of it. I just knew I needed to keep holding on to Jesus; I recited Bible verses to help me in the rough moments and tried to focus on one day at a time—sometimes even just one step at a time.

It was around this time that I also was contacted by the ACE rep in Australia about the need for help down under. I was immediately intrigued and called my parents.

"Hi, Mom, Dad. Guess what."

Dad's voice came over the line. "Well, and hello to you, too. Yes, we are doing okay, thank you very much."

"Ah, Dad, yeah, yeah. But guess what—I've heard they're looking for help in Australia. What do you think about that?"

"My first thought is that it's a long way away."

Mom's voice came over the extension. "However, it is an English-speaking country, which makes things easier if you're interested in going."

Dad continued. "You need to pray about it. You just came off a trip that you're still recovering from, so make sure this is what God wants for you. Have you spoken to the Alberta school about it?"

"No, I wanted to talk to you first."

"You really enjoy the people in Alberta. Are you sure you want to leave that all behind?" Mom always knew the hard questions to ask.

"Well, I've looked into it a bit and probably can go over for about six months. I don't know if the school would be willing to let me go for a year and then return."

"That might be the place to start. If they'll give you a sabbatical, then the first door has opened and you need to step through and see what God has next." Dad cleared his throat and continued. "And speaking of trips, your mother and I have been talking." I heard Mom's soft laugh.

"Really, what? Are you guys are planning a trip again?"

Since Dad didn't like to appear sentimental, his voice was gruff. "It was ten years ago that we took you on your graduation trip. Do you remember that?"

I laughed. "Of course. When you asked what I wanted for graduation, I said a trip to either Prince Edward Island or Alaska. So you took us on a six-week jaunt to PEI. It was great."

Dad continued. "We've had a rough couple of years, and you've been struggling. So we wondered if you'd like to go with us on your other option as a ten year post-grad gift?"

I nearly yelled into the phone. "Alaska? You're going to Alaska? Of course I want to go along."

Mom chuckled. "We sort of assumed that might be your answer. We're getting things sorted on the farm to be gone for six weeks from the middle of July to the end of August, if that works for you."

"Believe me, I'll make it work!"

We discussed a few details before I hung up the phone and looked at my calendar. After days of praying, planning, and checking finances, I decided that if I lived like Scrooge, I could make all these trips happen. My next step was to talk with Bert.

"Bert, I've been contacted about going to Australia if I can get into the country."

He took a sip of his coffee and glanced up. "Are you interested in going over the summer months, like you did with Peru?"

"With how expensive and how far it is, I'd need to go for longer. I think I can go in on a US passport for six months without a problem. So I have a proposition. If you'd be willing to let me have a sabbatical, then I'd be willing to commit to a two-year term here when I return."

"Well, I'd have to take it up at the next board meeting and see what they have to say."

We discussed some pros and cons for him to present for me. While waiting for the board's response, I contacted the Australian man again.

"I am definitely interested in coming if it works out. Where would you send me?"

He didn't have a direct answer for me. "There are several schools around Australia that could use help. When we get closer to the date, I'll make the final decision. Just buy a plane ticket to Sydney, our capital, and I'll take care of the rest of your travel to your final destination."

The school board agreed to my sabbatical, and other doors continued to open for going to Australia, so I was on an extremely limited budget for the year. When Belinda complained that I never wanted to do anything, I cheerfully remarked that I was happy to do without in the present to have fun in the future. Eventually I had saved enough for each trip and felt a great sense of fulfillment in meeting a tough challenge.

Chapter 23

The day came for me to fly out on trip number one. April Brown kindly took me into Edmonton that afternoon. I had a red-eye flight so spent several hours just hanging around the airport. That made it a long trip before I was finally able to meet Cheryl outside an Ontario airport. We had planned to use her small standard Honda Civic because it got great gas mileage.

Since I was so tired, she drove the first several hours while I pushed the seat back, relaxed, and visited. Somewhere in Quebec she and I switched places. Shortly thereafter, I entered a small town and stopped at the stoplight. Just as the light turned green—*wham*! My head jolted and I thought, *Oh my goodness! We just got rear-ended*. I turned to look at Cheryl. She was laughing.

"Wow, Cheryl! You are sure handling this well."

She grinned at me. "You certainly have lost your touch."

My jaw dropped. "Lost my touch? What on earth are you talking about?"

"For a farm girl, you've lost your touch driving a standard. You popped the clutch big-time, girl. You need to get back into the swing of it. That really jerked my head."

"Cheryl! I didn't pop the clutch. We were rear-ended."

"W-h-a-t?" Her laughter morphed into shock, and she fumbled with the seatbelt. "We've been rear-ended? Oh no!"

As we got out and met with the other driver, the fact that he spoke only French and we spoke only English complicated things a bit. Thankfully the damage wasn't bad, and since he was eager to give us more than enough money to cover the cost of the broken tail lights if we just let him go, we settled for that.

When we got close to the border, we decided to cut through Maine instead of travelling north and then back south to stay just in Canada. We had a slight holdup at the USA customs.

The lady inspector took a look at me. "What is your relation to this lady?" She pointed to Cheryl.

"She's my sister-in-law."

"Where's your permission slip?"

"My what?"

"I need to see the permission slip from your parents that she's allowed to take you out of the country."

I was stunned. "What on earth for?"

"All minors must have permission slips from parents, even if a child is travelling with extended family." Cheryl choked on her laughter while my face got red.

"Ma'am, I'm twenty-five. I don't need permission. I haven't lived at home for seven years."

Now it was the inspector's turn to be astonished. "Are you sure?"

I grimaced and pulled out my driver's license. "See? I can't help how I look; I'm really an adult." We soon were sent on our way, but Cheryl enjoyed making me squirm over that little incident.

In Maine we drove on a narrow, twisting, winding road that was a fun, roller coaster ride. By the time we made it back into New Brunswick, I was ready to stop for the night; however, we had to detour, as the roads were blocked by "clam bed" protesters.

I looked at Cheryl. "What's a clam bed protester?"

"I have no idea, but it doesn't look as if we're going to be able to get through here. Look at all the picketers!"

"This is the first time I've ever seen a big, stop-the-traffic group of people marching around with their signs." I rolled down my window, and one of the protesters walked over. "Excuse me, sir. I'm from Alberta and hope to enjoy a chance to visit your wonderful province. Is there a different way we could go to get to Fredericton?"

He very nicely gave me a couple options and we backed up, turned around, and headed on our way. Cheryl gave me a wry grin. "You certainly don't hesitate to talk to people. What would you have done if he'd been angry and aggressive?"

I shot her a cheeky smirk. "I would have 'clammed' up!"

Once we'd enjoyed some seafood and sightseeing in New Brunswick, we continued on toward the coast and found the ferry for Newfoundland. At the ticket booth we were a bit shocked at the price.

"Cheryl, are you sure we want to go? That's $152 per person just to get over there, and we can't take the car. If we do, that's another sum of money."

"But Stacy, this is the only province you haven't been in yet. You're close to meeting that goal you set when you graduated, about getting to every state and province in North America by the time you're thirty."

"But this is too much for just a quick trip. We could see a lot of other things for that amount of money instead of just one place. Maybe I'll fly into it someday. This summer I'll get into Alaska and the Yukon, so that's already another couple of places I can tick off my list."

"Well, if you're sure."

"Yes, I am. Where should we go instead?"

"How about Prince Edward Island?"

"Oh, yes. I loved that place when my parents took me there."

We turned the car around and headed off toward PEI. That was the nice thing about this trip. There was no set destination; we could wander as we wished. We also worked well together. I hated city driving, which Cheryl was fine with, and I loved navigating, which was not Cheryl's cup of tea. So I did the country driving, and she took on the cities while I held the map and directed.

By the time we arrived at the ferry in Nova Scotia, we had a burned-out headlight. Since we had just missed the ferry, we had an hour to wait for the next one. That gave us time to replace the headlight. Crossing in April was so different from my summer crossing ten years previously. The ice was all around us, and the crashing sound of the big ferry plowing through it gave me the shivers. The biting wind pricked my cheeks as we walked along the perimeter, peering down into the icy blackness. Many thoughts of the *Titanic* floated through my mind as my imagination took flight of what that fateful journey must have been like.

The few days we spent on the island were special. Cheryl didn't like to take the same road twice, so we covered a lot of area with our driving. I enjoy roaming through cemeteries, and PEI was dotted with them. At first we couldn't understand why such a small place would have so many graveyards, but when I bought a map of the cemeteries, I realized it was because of all the shipwrecks. The history you could read between the lines as you looked at gravestones fascinated me.

Of course, Cavendish, with Anne of Green Gables, was a must. Since it was off-season, I knew we couldn't get in, but at least we could look around. However, when we pulled into the parking lot, I noticed a single car there.

"Hey, Cheryl, look! We aren't the only people here." I craned my neck around. "But I don't see anyone anywhere."

"Maybe they went down Lover's Lane. There's a sign pointing that direction."

"Let's go look in the windows." I scrambled out of the car and headed up to the green-gabled house. Peering in the window, I nearly jumped out of my skin. "Aaaah!"

Cheryl rushed up. "What's wrong?"

"I saw a face!" Just then the door creaked open and I jumped again. A body to add to the face appeared in the doorway.

"May I help you?" The lady was a tour guide who was giving a family from Japan a special, pre-arranged, off-season tour. When the family heard we had driven here from Ontario after I flew in from Alberta, they invited us to join them, and we split the cost. That was extra-special for me because we had the house to ourselves instead of packed with various tourists. I could pretend I was Anne running up to her bedroom, or dreaming her fanciful dreams.

Once the lady and the family had left, we headed back to Lover's Lane. Since it was full of snow, it wasn't as fanciful a place. At first the snow was crusty and I could walk on top, but then it suddenly gave way, and I sank in and almost got stuck.

"Ha. Anne didn't know what she was talking about. Lover's Lane is not all that wonderful!" I pulled my boot out of the snow and dumped the icy stuff out. "Let's head back."

When we were done on PEI, we headed for the ferry. We timed it just right and were the fourth last car to board, so we pulled out without any waiting. I met one of the workers and found out they could hold ninety-five cars on our deck, while almost that many trucks were on the lower deck.

We had fun in a few picturesque places in Nova Scotia and New Brunswick as we headed west once again. After checking our wallets, our time, and our distance, we made the decision to try and see Niagara Falls before returning to

Cochrane and Cheryl's home. Once again we dipped down into the States for some serious driving. We cut through Maine, New Hampshire, and Vermont. We were pushing to make it back across the border into Quebec before stopping for the night. I was at the wheel when something rolled across the road right in front of the car. I swerved but still hit it and—*kgrrcstck*. A horrible sound eddied forth from the back end of the car. We stopped and saw that the muffler had broken off. Thankfully we were able to find the part in one piece and stuck it in the trunk. But the muffled roar as we drove up to customs was unnerving. I prayed that we wouldn't have trouble, but they let us in without comment about our loud sounds.

God was good. When we pulled into the nearest town and found a motel, there was a garage right beside it. The next morning the man kindly soldered the muffler back on for us for just $13.00. As we pulled out again, Cheryl looked at me.

"I've had this car for seven years and barely did anything other than change the oil. In the one week we've been together, I've had a new headlight, new taillights, and now a muffler put on. You are a magnet for adventures. What next?"

The "what next" was getting lost in Montreal for an hour. Since Cheryl was at the wheel, I told her she couldn't blame that on me.

"But you're with me, and I've never been lost in Montreal before," was her retort.

"Ha. Have you ever been to Montreal before?" Her grin gave me my answer.

Going through Toronto was easier than I expected. We must have hit it at just the right time because the traffic wasn't bad. We drove past the CN Tower and managed to arrive in Niagara Falls that afternoon with no further problems. Finding a motel wasn't a problem because it was off-season, so there were vacancies. We chose one with a pool for our last special hurrah.

The daffodils and crocuses were just pushing themselves up from the flowerbeds, and the feel of spring was lovely as we wandered around looking at the falls, sightseeing, and souvenir shopping. In the evening we went to a special restaurant and watched the beautiful light display over the falls. It was a memorable evening.

The next morning we took an early-morning swim before anyone was around. Then we packed our bags and checked out. We did a bit more sightseeing before heading to the car to pull out on our journey once again. Cheryl kept giving me these strange looks and then smirking. Finally I couldn't take it anymore.

"What's wrong with you? Why do you keep looking at me?"

She struggled to hold in her laughter. "I'm not sure how to tell you this."

"Tell me what?"

"You know how you're so sensitive to things?"

"Yeah, so what?"

"I'm wondering if they put chemical stuff in the pool that doesn't suit your skin."

I was puzzled. "Why?"

She choked on a bit of laughter. "I'm sorry, but you are kinda changing colour."

"W-h-a-a-t?" I jerked the car mirror around to look in it. Sure enough, my face looked like it was sunburnt with blotchy shades of red and pink, while my hair had almost orangey streaks straggling through it. "Oh no!" I scowled at her. "How come I'm changing colour when you look fine. You were in the pool, too."

She burst out laughing and leaned against the car. "Like I said, you're the magnet for adventure, not me. But don't worry. For most of the day, we'll just be in the car travelling, so no one will see you much."

Eight days after we set off on our adventures, we drove back into her yard again. We had driven approximately 5,500 kilometres (3,400 miles) and seen a lot of God's wonderful creation over a distance covering five Canadian provinces and three of the USA states.

One of the things that caught me by surprise was how hard it was to be in Nick's house without him there. I kept expecting him to walk through the door. A wave of grief rolled over me every time I realized that wouldn't happen. That night I had one of my nightmares again; this time Nick was in Peru with me, and I didn't save him. I woke up crying, and it gave me a glimpse into what Cheryl had to go through living in the house alone. I realized once again grief is an ongoing road to travel. I couldn't just cross a finish line and be done with that part of my life. But it also helped to see that as time went on, good times stayed a bit longer and pushed the sad times farther apart.

On Sunday Cheryl let me borrow the car to go out to Hunta. I wanted to see the people again in the church where Dad had been a preacher. Our arrival the previous night occurred in a snow flurry. From spring and daffodils in the east to snow and cold in the north—Canada has a wide variety in its seasons. That snow had melted overnight, making her yard a bit of a quagmire. As I backed out of the yard, I got stuck. Cheryl was laughing as she came out of the house to help me push.

I glowered at her. "Don't even say it."

"Say what?"

"What I see quivering on the tip of your tongue. This mud mess has nothing to do with me!" I puffed and panted as we shoved and pushed to get it onto firmer ground.

"But only you would back right into it. If you'd stayed more to the left, that ground is still hard." She gave one last heave and the wheels left the mud with a mighty slurp. The splatter of mud, or course, landed right on my skirt.

"Oh, great. Now I've got to change."

Cheryl just grinned. "Next time don't back into the mud. You and your adventures."

Since I'd planned to leave early to visit, I wasn't late for church. It was good to see everyone and get caught up on all the news.

In the afternoon we visited with some of Cheryl's family and then took a trip out to the cemetery to see Nick's tombstone. As twilight fell, we returned to the house so I could pack.

Monday morning was our last drive together as we headed to the airport. It was so hard to say goodbye to Cheryl. We'd had a good week both crying and laughing together as we shared in our grief as well as in the fun moments of the trip.

Chapter 24

Back at school, I had a busy last quarter getting the school year finished up and making sure the next year's order, the records, and everything else were in tiptop shape. People seemed strangely reticent to talk when I asked if they'd found someone to fill in for my sabbatical, but I didn't think much about it. I was busy trying to decide what to pack and leave at a farm for next year, what to keep out for Alaska, and what I'd need for Australia besides the things needed for the two-day drive home.

It was harder to pack for so many trips than I expected, but I managed to get everything finished, stored, and loaded into my car by my deadline Sunday. After the service I went around shaking hands, telling everyone I'd see them in a year. As I left the building, Bert and another parent called me aside and told me the news everyone had been keeping from me.

"By the way, I need to tell you that we found another girl willing to come teach here." Bert didn't look at me as he talked.

I smiled. "Oh, that's great. That makes me feel so much better. I hated to leave you in the lurch if you couldn't find someone."

"Yes, well, the thing is—she wants to come for a two-year term. She didn't want to commit to less."

As I stared at the men in shock, it took a minute for the news to sink in. Then waves of humiliation rolled over me as I suddenly understood the strange looks people kept giving me when I said my goodbyes. I was the only one who hadn't known I wasn't coming back. The next emotion to rush through me was anger over all the unneeded packing and storing I'd done based on my return in a year. Finally, the feeling of betrayal hit hard. Had they told me about this when they first interviewed her, I'd have gladly stepped down. I knew I was leaving them, and my offer to return for two years was to help them, not create problems for them. But to let me be ignorant until fifteen hours before I drove away—that burned deep down into my soul. My pride took a hit at the humiliation of looking like a fool in front of the whole church with my "see you next year" attitude, but the deep-down hurt was that people who were like family to me could treat me like that. Maybe they didn't know how to address it and didn't want to hurt me by rescinding the agreement we'd made, but allowing me to continue in ignorance of my changed status until I was ready to leave was a slap in the face. The betrayal felt so intense I had to grab the handrail to keep from staggering.

Bert stretched his hand toward me and I cringed away. "Is there anything you want to ask?"

My voice quivered embarrassingly. "What's there to say?" I turned and ran down the steps. I heard him calling after me, but I couldn't stop. I needed to get home before I completely fell to pieces. I locked myself in my bedroom and cried all afternoon. Belinda was the only one I let in. She was indignant on my behalf, which was a small comfort. I know April came to my door a couple times saying someone was on the phone for me, but I just couldn't talk to anyone, nor eat, the entire afternoon. My plan had been to leave by 5:00 Monday morning, but I was so distraught that I couldn't sleep. When the clock showed 2:00 a.m., I decided I might as well leave. My car was already packed, so I just needed to dress and slip out the door. I left a farewell note on the table for the Browns and hit the road.

The two-day drive was a struggle. I had to pull over several times, as I was crying too hard to see the road. I talked to God a lot over those hours.

God, why? Why did they do it like that?

Child, everyone is human. People make mistakes.

But why didn't they just tell me right off someone wanted to come for more than a year?

People don't always know how to discuss things. You're not good with confrontations. You weren't willing to talk to anyone yesterday.

That's different. I couldn't talk without crying. Had they told me their problem, I would have gladly stepped down.

Did you tell them that?
Well, no, but they never asked.
So they didn't tell you something you needed to know, and you never mentioned stuff maybe they needed to know.
But God, I feel like a fool. All those goodbyes.
Now that's pride talking.
I feel so betrayed. I thought they were my friends.
Remember Jesus and Judas.

When I finally arrived at home, I had to explain the whole hurtful story to my parents. Mom gave me motherly comfort, while Dad was more practical.

"Have a good cry and get it out of your system, and then start looking forward at the good."

I stared at him. "What's good about it? If it wasn't to be, then why agree to have me back in the first place?"

He looked at me. "Stacy, you put out a fleece when you were praying about Australia. You said if Mayerthorpe agreed to have you back for two years, you'd take it as a sign you should go to Australia. God gave that sign you asked for, but He never promised it would stay. It was needed at the time to keep you proceeding with paperwork for overseas. If you expect God to lead and guide, then you need to accept that your plans aren't always His plans. If the Mayerthorpe door is closing, then there's something different for you after Australia. God will reveal it in His time. You just trust and hang on."

I took a shuddery breath. "Yeah, okay, but does it have to hurt so much?"

Mom passed me a tissue. "Betrayal is extremely painful. But having gone through it, you will have compassion for people in ways you didn't have before." Then she smiled. "Our trip to Alaska will be a good thing for you, too. It will help take your mind off things."

Dad added the final comments. "As much as you're hurting right now, Stacy, remember there are two sides to every story. Right now you can only see your side. We don't know what combination of things occurred with the school to have them handle the situation the way they did. They have been good to you over the years, and you don't want to lose that friendship. Your mom's right. This trip will take your mind off things, and with time and distance, clarity is easier. Give your hurt to God and look forward, not back."

I knew he was right, but I was feeling raw. "Can I at least have a pity party first?"

He gave me his "dad" look. "Just make sure you're over it by lunchtime. I need you to help me get the hay crop off this week before we leave."

Because of the stress, the lack of sleep, and the many tears I shed, I came down with a horrible cold. The next week as we finished haying and worked on the van to prepare for Alaska, I was feeling downright miserable. Of course that was not going to stop me from taking this trip.

Chapter 25

We had the van packed and loaded and were ready to pull out. For this trip Dad had made a small, two-wheeled trailer to pull behind the van. Since he loved going down the back roads to explore, he wanted to have a lot of tools and a few spare tires along. He placed the tires flat and laid a big board over them. Then we flung a pad on top. I also tossed in my tent. That gave me three options for sleeping—on a board across the two front seats like I normally did, with my leg stuck through the steering wheel so I didn't fall off in the night, or on the board in the little trailer, or in my tent. Six weeks can be a long time of togetherness for four people in a van 24/7, so I was happy with my options. What I was not so happy about was that my sister stuck to me like a leech. If I slept in the van then she did, too. If I was in the trailer, she wanted to be there. When I set up my tent, she tried to persuade me to allow her to sleep there. It annoyed me to no end. I needed some space after what I'd endured in the past year or so, while she needed reassurance that she wasn't going to lose her sister like she had her brother, and I didn't recognize that. It made for a few interesting moments as we tried to adjust to each other again.

Late in the afternoon on July 13, we officially left our yard and drove just a short way to get a good start on the adventures that would befall us. The next day being Julie's birthday, we stopped in Portage to visit friends and celebrate her birthday by having cake with them. From there our next stop was a farm in Saskatchewan that Dad was interested in. We'd been at the Ridgeville farm a number of years, so Dad was starting to look at farms again.

When we arrived in Edmonton, Dad shocked me by taking us to the

West Edmonton Mall. He wasn't a city person; the logging roads and wildlife beckoned to him way more than touristy stuff. But he came in with us and we had a lovely few hours watching the dolphin show, stopping at the waterpark where people were bungy jumping, and venturing into Fantasyland. Looking back, I wonder if he made an extra-special effort to do things he had no interest in on my behalf.

We stayed overnight in Mayerthorpe for two reasons. I wanted to see Belinda again, and by the time we got there, I felt so ill that I was willing to go to the hospital to be checked. I couldn't believe it when the doctor said he wanted to test for mono. But I shuffled into the exam room and waited. A young man came in and what followed was a bit of a nightmare.

My fear of needles and doctors and hospitals came rushing to the forefront as the poor guy collapsed vein after vein trying to get a needle into me. He tried the right arm, the left arm, back to the right. Each time I got more agitated and fearful. He got a couple of vials of blood but kept saying he needed more. I don't know if I went into shock, but puddles of sweat were pouring from me. He tried to put a bandage on the needle punctures and it floated right off my arm. I got so lightheaded, I keeled over. He forced me to get on a stretcher while he ran for help. I overheard him say something about strapping me on the stretcher as he left, and that pushed my panic button. As soon as he was gone, I crawled off the stretcher, grabbed my belongings, and headed out the door. I made it outside without being caught. I didn't care if I was at death's door; I was not dying in the hospital. I staggered down the street like a drunken sailor. It was two blocks to the Browns' house. I made it only one block before I keeled over again.

It's amazing what sheer grit and determination can do. Somehow I managed to get on my hands and knees and crawled the rest of the way. My teeth were chattering I was so cold, yet I still had sweat pouring off me. I was just thankful no one was around to see me. When I crawled up their driveway, I didn't have the strength to reach up for the doorknob. I just huddled against the door frame, shivering and shaking. When April opened the door sometime later to come out, she shrieked as I fell into the hall.

"Stacy? What on earth has happened to you? Do I need to call an ambulance?"

"N-o-o, n-o-o!" I stuttered and stammered. "No hospital. That's what made me like this. I'll die here, but don't take me back there." That's the last

I remember for quite some time.

When I came to, I was lying in bed in their guest room, and my parents were sitting beside me. Mom sighed. "Stacy, you gave us such a fright. We left you at the hospital while we went for some groceries. When we came back, they said you had disappeared, and they didn't know where you went. What happened?"

"That man. He kept sticking me and sticking me. I couldn't take it anymore."

"The good news is he got enough blood to see that you don't have mono."

When Mom didn't look me in the eyes, I got suspicious.

"What's the bad news?"

"They think you should go in for more tests."

I sat straight up. "Not on your life! I'll either live or die. They don't have to test me for that." Since I was an adult, no one could force me to go back. We stayed an extra day for me to rest, and I was right. I did live.

We pulled out the day after, and I was happy to be on the road. I gradually felt better, although I had massive bruising on both arms from the needles, and a resurgence of paranoia about needles and hospitals.

When we hit the Northwest Territories boundary lines, we got a certificate about crossing the 60th parallel. That night we stayed around Hay River and found out that the Manitoba mosquitoes had nothing on these monster skeeters. They were brutal.

At Fort Providence we used the ferry to cross the Mackenzie River and camp there. The wind was so biting we had to put on our warmest clothes. Jocelyn was not impressed.

"This is the middle of summer. I should not have to wear my winter jacket in July." Her lips were blue-ish as we huddled close.

"There's one good thing, though." I shivered a bit, but not as much as she.

"What could that be?"

"With this cold, nasty wind, the mosquitoes aren't biting!"

"I think I'd rather have that."

"I wouldn't. You just don't get bit like I do." I scowled at her. I'd always had more problems with mosquitoes than she did. "I already have fifteen bites just on one leg."

We stopped at a church for Sunday and found out they were holding a baptism at the river, so after church we attended that. The wind was strong enough at the river that we didn't have mosquitoes, but when we returned to the church building, they were so thick you had to use a fly swatter to sweep off the screen door before quickly dashing in. One mosquito makes a tiny whiny sound. A huge, dark cloud of them sounded like a mini-jackhammer.

I believe that today most of the Alaska Highway is paved, but at that time only a section of it was, so we hit gravel about three hundred miles up and had a dusty drive the rest of the way. We bought *The Mile Post*, a book about points of interest along the Alaskan Highway. I was astonished at the traffic despite the gravel. At Fort Nelson we saw a caravan of fifteen RVs making their way along. Another place had thirty of them. However, the farther we went, the more spread out the traffic became until finally we'd spend most of the day alone without another vehicle in sight.

Watson Lake was incredible. I hadn't known about the famous Signpost boardwalk. I was so disappointed that we hadn't brought a license plate to hang on those posts that stretched for blocks. Signs were tacked on from around the world. Mom surrendered one of her tinfoil pie pans to the cause, and I used it to punch out our name and placed it among all the other signs people had put up. The other not-so-incredible part about Watson Lake was that by the time I finished nailing the sign on, I had obtained forty-seven mosquito bites. None of my family had as many issues as I did with those nasty bugs. They had lots of t-shirts along the way that proclaimed, "I gave blood in _____." After the name of the place was a picture of a big mosquito. At the rate I was going, I was donating blood in every town along the route as well as in the wilderness areas.

My twenty-sixth birthday was spent in Whitehorse. It was a great day. We toured a few places, which even Dad enjoyed, as the things we saw were historic. My favourite place was the SS *Klondike*, which was the last restored paddlewheel boat used in the Klondike Gold Rush of 1898. Mom had brought a canned chicken, cranberry sauce, and creamed corn along for a supper treat. We finished off my birthday supper with a chocolate roll.

We camped outside Whitehorse that evening by a river that had pavement alongside it, so while Dad changed oil, Jocelyn and I tried playing tennis. We had to imagine the net and sidelines, and it was a bit difficult, as we were on a slope, but we had fun.

As I lay down to sleep that night, I reviewed my past few birthdays. *Lord, life sure changes. My twenty-fourth birthday we had a family reunion* in Manitoba—*the last time I saw my brother alive. For my twenty-fifth, I had a Spanish fiesta in Peru amidst friends and danger. Now here I've turned twenty-six in the Yukon Territory touring a gold rush boat. What will the twenty-seventh one be like?*

My child, your times are in My hands. I never promised an easy life, but remember that My grace is sufficient for you.

I certainly can't complain of boredom, Lord!

Life goes through seasons just like the weather does. Trust Me.

I try, Lord, but lately I feel overwhelmed. My future was nicely planned out, and now I'm left hanging.

I know the plans I have for you, Child. You will never be out of My care. Have faith to step out and leave the planning to Me.

I rolled over and decided to do my best not to think past Australia. In six months, I'd worry about the next step.

Dawson was our next major stop. I'd been looking forward to seeing this place, as I'd read Jack London's books and loved Robert Service's poetry. One of my first stops was to see their cabins and buy a book of Service's best poetry.

The city was left to look like it had in 1898. Poor Mother just assumed it was all facades and was mortified when she took us into a saloon, only to find it really was a saloon. She hustled us out of there in fine fashion, but we teased her for weeks about it.

When we left Dawson, I was at the wheel so Dad could have a rest. I didn't realize what the Top-of-the-World-Highway was going to be like, and was rather nervous about some of the steep drop-offs. With rolling gravel it was easy to slide if you picked up any speed, so I just poked along. It was a relief when he woke up so that he could take over, although I'd never admit that to him. He and I switched off frequently as we made our way along, but he usually did the hard places. I usually drove over lunchtime so I could eat first, which took him a long time to figure out. We always had supper and breakfast outside after stopping for the night and before leaving in the morning, but lunch was sandwiches, chips, and veggies eaten in the van while travelling. In our family it was tradition that the one who was driving got fed first. Jocelyn was the one who snitched about my secret.

"Hey, Dad, it's 11:00. You've been driving a few hours. Why don't we switch off so you can stretch out?" I nudged his shoulder. We made the switch and

I heard Jocelyn snicker.

Dad looked at her. "What's the joke?"

She grinned. "Don't you get what Stacy's doing?" I glared at her, but she ignored me.

Dad frowned thoughtfully. "No. What do you think?"

"She always tells you she's not ready to drive first thing in the morning."

"And what has that to do with anything?"

Jocelyn smirked at me. "So then she's always at the wheel when it's time for lunch."

Mother looked puzzled. "Why is that a problem?"

I tried to distract them from the conversation. "Hey, look, is that an animal?"

Jocelyn would not be deterred. "It's not, but who gets the first sandwich for lunch? The driver. And just who happens to be driving every lunchtime?"

I saw the light go on in everyone's mind. I turned red.

Mom giggled. "Stacy. For shame!"

Dad mocked-glared at me. "God gave you a brain, but not to use it for your own self-satisfaction!" However, we'd established a good routine for driving by then, so I still got to do most of the lunchtime driving. I wouldn't let Jocelyn sleep in the tent with me that night after ratting on me like that, though.

Chicken, Alaska, was our entry point into Alaska from the Top-of-the-World-Highway. I'd read the book *Tisha*, so was intrigued by this little village. While Dad did some work on the van, Jocelyn and I took the pans left on the porch trading post to go down to the stream and try our hand at gold mining. It took me only a few minutes to decide those gold rush dudes had to be insane. The water was freezing cold, it was back-breaking to stand hunched over a gold pan, and how to swirl the water without losing everything in it was a mystery.

There were a couple old-timers sitting in the rocking chairs watching us. Soon one of them came down to us. He nudged me.

"Not like that." He held out his hand for the pan. I handed it over and he scooped up a pan full of silt and gravel. "Like this." He started to gently swirl the water. He wasn't talkative but was very patient as he showed me the proper way to pan for gold.

"Like this?" I tried and swished water over me.

"No. Slower." He put his hand over mine to lessen my speed.

I grinned. "I'm not big on patience."

"Then you won't find gold."

Because of his help, I actually found a sliver of gold. I offered it to him. "Here. You earned this. I'd never have gotten the hang of it."

"Keep it. Put it on a piece of tape so you don't lose it."

Jocelyn was fascinated by it. "It's so tiny. Is it real gold? Is it worth anything?"

The man straightened. "Yep. Yep. 'Bout three dollars."

He looked at me. "Keep it. Remember, gold is hard work, just like anything worthwhile."

"Yes, sir." He walked away. Later someone approached me.

"I heard Old Jim actually helped you pan for gold!"

I shrugged. "I don't know his name, but yes, someone showed me some tips."

"How did you get him to actually do that?"

I stared in surprise. "Nothing. He just came down and helped. Why?"

The man cocked his head. "He's a true old-timer who settled in this area during the Depression and found some gold. I'm a journalist. I've been trying for days to talk to him and get his story, but he's a bit of a hermit and I can't get near him. What did you do?"

I shook my head again. "Honestly, nothing. He was rocking in that chair and I smiled at him when my sister and I walked by to get the pans. Then he came and joined us at the river."

The man threw up his hands in frustration and walked away.

We stopped in Fairbanks to stock up on supplies before we headed for Denali Park. That was the biggest tourist area we encountered on the trip. The bus tours through the park were all full for the day, so we couldn't get on until Tuesday noon. We spent the day doing various things, such as watching the dog sled demonstrations. We were even allowed to walk in the kennels and see the dogs.

Of course I had questions. "Excuse me, sir, but why do you always bring your dogs out on two legs? Doesn't that seem awkward?"

He laughed. "These dogs are trained to pull fully loaded sleds. They are powerful animals and eager to work."

I frowned. "They're hopping like Easter bunnies."

"If we let them down on all fours, they'd pull us right off our feet." He grinned at me as my eyebrows shot up.

"Oh, my, I never thought about that." I blushed when he laughed again.

"Believe me, you get pulled off your feet and dragged only once. You never forget to let them walk with only two feet when getting ready to hitch them up."

Jocelyn, Dad, and I decided to hike up to the Mt. Healy Outlook. Mom had a heart condition so just stayed at the van with her books and puzzles. As we picked up a brochure about the hike, I noticed a bunch of small bells for sale.

"What are all these bells?"

The sales clerk answered. "Some people like to buy them to tie them on their shoes when hiking."

Jocelyn jumped in. "Why?"

The clerk held a pair out to her. "To scare the bears away. If they hear noise, they usually avoid people in most circumstances. Would you like to buy these?"

Jocelyn shook her head. "Nah, don't need them. We have my sister."

Now it was the clerk's turn to look puzzled. "What has that to do with it?"

Jocelyn grinned at me. "My sister is always singing. That's enough to scare any bear away." My face went bright red as the clerk laughed.

I did sing my way up the mountain. When we reached the top, Jocelyn looked at me.

"Well, you should be happy. Not only did you scare the bears away, but all the people, too. We haven't met a single soul on the trip up."

Thankfully on the way down we did meet a few people headed for the outlook, or she would have never let me forget it.

Our bus tour the next day was neat. The driver told us we were lucky.

"Many times people come out here and don't see much. We never know when the animals are roaming. It's not often we see so much all in one day." By the end of our tour, we'd seen ptarmigan, squirrel, fox, caribou, two wolves, and three grizzlies. I wasn't sure why people exclaimed so over the grizzlies. I thought they looked rather ugly. I turned to Jocelyn.

"Hmm. What's the fuss? I think Limpy and Growly were much more handsome than these guys are."

Jocelyn nodded. "Our Ontario bears were much cleaner than these ones."

After Denali, we arrived in Anchorage and got held up in traffic by a moose. He was being very stubborn about moving, and they finally had to get officers in to deal with him.

The Kenai peninsula was far busier than we expected. The fishing season was on, and there were so many fishermen in the river, I'm not sure how they caught anything except each other. Since none of us were huge crowd people, we moved on. We spent quite a bit of time in Palmer, as Dad was interested in some dairy farms in the area. While he talked to farmers, we girls spent our time at some garage sales and a library.

Finally we turned the van around and started the long trek back toward home. At one point we passed an Air Stream parked along the side of the road. Since Dad always stopped to help people, it was nothing unusual that he stopped on this occasion. This family had three bolts sheared off their rear wheel. We spent the day finding a hermit's place because he had a wrecking yard. During this process we discovered the Air Stream driver had actually gone to school with Dad's oldest brother. They were from Michigan, we were from Manitoba, and we met in the wilds of Alaska.

It took us hours to locate the hermit people told us about. Everyone knew about him, but no one knew where he actually lived. I was grateful that when Dad actually tracked him down in the middle of nowhere, he had an outhouse.

"Dad, ask him if I can use his outhouse," I whispered out the van window as Dad walked over to talk to the hermit. Since we now had a family of three in the van with us, I didn't want to just use nature. Upon receiving a gruff nod of permission, I gingerly made my way over to the dilapidated outhouse. I opened the door and stared in amazement at the weeds growing up through the hole. I turned around and headed for the van.

"Mom, may I borrow the scissors?"

Mom stuck her head out the window. "Scissors? Why do you need scissors?"

Her voice drew everyone's attention and I turned red. "Never mind, just pass me the scissors." With the amount of grass, a sickle would have been a much better option, but we didn't carry that.

With the day's delay, we pushed hard to get back down into Canada. The Whitehorse tourist centre had given us special passports to get stamped as we travelled to the different places in the Yukon and Alaska. Since we managed to get all nine places stamped, when we returned to Whitehorse, we received a poster about intrepid travellers.

Most of the drive north had been relaxing, just doing what we wanted, but now we were focused on getting home. We did stop at the national parks in Alberta to see Jasper, Banff, and Lake Louise. We hiked the Sundance Canyon and walked the Marsh Loop before continuing on. We dropped down into

Montana to get cheaper gas on the drive east. It was so hot after such cold nights in Alaska that one night we ate just ice cream for our supper.

We wearily and happily pulled into our driveway the middle of August, leaving me a week to get unpacked from this trip and ready to fly out on the next adventure.

Chapter 26

My countdown week to takeoff was slightly crazy. Not only were we busy unloading and settling back home, but I was still waiting to hear what I was supposed to do upon my arrival in Sydney, Australia. I couldn't get through to the man. On top of that, we had the second cutting of hay to bring in, so I didn't have time to worry about much.

Two days before departure I finally connected with someone in the ACE office in Australia. I couldn't talk with the man in charge, but the lady told me he'd left a message.

"When you get to Sydney, there will be a lady named Julia waiting for you. She'll have your tickets. She's tall with black hair."

I couldn't hear well because of the connection. "Sorry, what about my tickets? Where am I being sent?"

Static crossed the wires. "Julia ... info ... ok." The line went dead. Mom had been listening to my end of the conversation.

"Is everything sorted out?"

I hung up the phone. "I think so. Someone named Julia will have tickets to somewhere for me."

Mom frowned. "That sounds a bit vague to fly thousands of miles on."

I shrugged. "Oh well, what could go wrong? At least I'll be in an English-speaking country."

My D-day quickly arrived, and everyone came along to take me to the airport. Again, I made them just drop me and leave once I knew my tickets were in order to fly. I didn't want the prolonged farewell.

This flight took me to Vancouver, where I switched planes to go to Honolulu. From there I was pleased when I boarded my ten-hour flight to Sydney to discover I had a row of seats to myself. Those long hauls are dreadful when you're crammed three in a row. Before I could spread out, another girl jammed into the middle seat in her row slipped over into my empty seat so I had to share. But at least we had a space between us for wiggle room. I can't sit still even in my own house, so ten hours on a plane is torture both for myself and anyone sitting in my vicinity.

Customs was a breeze. I had no trouble going through, but once I'd collected my luggage and exited into the main terminal, I suddenly realized I had a problem. My Winnipeg International Airport and the Sydney one were like a mouse and an elephant in comparison size-wise. I looked at massive numbers of people surging in all directions, and Mom's concern about vague instructions came floating back into my head.

Lord, help! There are thousands of people, and corridors in every direction. How on earth am I going to find a person named Julia in this?

I started approaching every dark-haired tall lady. "Excuse me, is your name Julia?" Most people were polite, although a few looked at me strangely. After twenty minutes of panic, I finally decided to calm down.

Stacy, take it easy. You arrived at 6:30 a.m. You have space to walk, toilets, and freedom to talk. If by noon no one has come for you, then you may panic.

I wandered up and down a few corridors and then finally sat down on the floor in one corridor and talked to the Lord.

Lord, help! What is going on? No one is here. My ticket is open-ended, but I have to stay a minimum of seven days. I have no Australian money. What am I to do?
Wait.
I've waited. It's been a couple hours now.
Wait.
I'm tired, Lord. I'm scared.
Wait.
All right, fine, Lord, but I'm not happy. I blew my breath out in frustration and plopped down on the floor. I pulled a book out of my bag and started to read. Suddenly from the corner of my eye, I saw two women race in and stare around wildly. One was tall and black-haired.

Really, Lord? You wait until I finally settle down and start to read, and <u>then</u>

bring them in? You have a strange sense of humour.

You need to learn to trust Me.

I sighed. *Yeah, Lord, You're right. Sorry.*

I got up and approached the two women. "Excuse me, are you looking for a Stacy Kanner from Canada?"

The women literally sagged in relief. The dark-haired one spoke. "I'm so sorry. I'm Julia. I've never driven in Sydney before, and we got lost."

The other one stuck out her hand. "I'm Darla. Thank you for not leaving on us."

Julia laughed. "Darla, we have her tickets. She can't leave without us."

"Oh, yeah, right." We all laughed.

I held out my hand. "So where am I going?"

The ladies looked at each other in bewilderment. "We don't know," Julia answered, passing over an envelope. "We were just told to meet you at the International Airport, give you this envelope, and take you over to the domestic terminal."

Darla piped up. "Don't you know where you're going? And you flew all this way?"

I shrugged and ripped open the envelope. We all peered at the tickets I pulled out. One was for Melbourne and the other said Devonport, Tasmania. I looked at the ladies. "Where's that?"

They both shrugged. "Tasmania is our island state. It's not large, but I have no idea where Devonport is." Darla looked at Julia, who also shook her head.

"Well, what do I do when I get to wherever this is?" I rolled my eyes when they informed me they didn't know.

Julia patted my shoulder. "I'm sure they'll have someone there to greet you and let you know what's next, just like they did here."

As she ushered me toward the exit and their car, I glanced up.

Lord! What next?

A step at a time, child.

After arriving at the domestic terminal and checking in, the ladies treated me to a lemonade. As we visited, Darla showed me what Australian money looked like. I exclaimed over the two-dollar coin, as I'd never seen such before. When I handed it back, she refused to take it.

"Keep it. You might want to buy a coffee in Melbourne between flights."

I sighed. "You really have no idea where I might be going?"

Darla frowned thoughtfully. "I think I remember meeting someone at a conference once from Tasmania. I believe she mentioned coming from Geneva. I remember it because I thought she meant Switzerland, but she had an Aussie accent."

Julia added her comfort. "Tasmania isn't a big island, and there aren't any big cities except for Hobart, so you shouldn't have trouble finding anyone."

The ladies said their goodbyes and left me at the departure gate. Since I still had time to pass, I started exploring, pulling my carry-on. I went up and down the corridors. On the last corridor, I spied a very weird spinning door.

Oh, cool! I gotta try this. It's going backwards from anything in Canada.

I left my bag by the door and started to push. I just wanted to make it spin me around once, and then I'd head for my gate. But Mom's voice droned insistently in my head. *Never leave your bag alone.* I argued. *Mom, just one spin. It's only ten seconds.* Her voice wouldn't leave my head. *Never leave your bag alone.* I sighed and turned around and grabbed my handle. *I hope you're happy.*

I jumped on the rotunda thingy and with a gigantic push sailed halfway around. Then I came to an abrupt stop. Frowning, I pushed on the door. *B-l-l-l-e-e-e-p-p-p.* An aggravating beeper blared while a metallic voice intoned, "This is a no-entry zone. You must back out and go through the proper channels to enter the airport." I looked over my shoulder and to my horror discovered I was on the *outside* of the airport. I shoved the door again, only to receive the same embarrassing beeper and voice. I looked down the long, long length of the building, grabbed my bag, and started running. As I ran, I thought, *Oops, Mom. Sorry. Guess you were right! SO glad I have my bag now!*

By the time I managed to get to the front of the airport and go through radar again, I was getting panicky that I'd miss my flight. Then to make matters worse, the officer on duty recognized me.

"Didn't I check you through here a couple hours ago?"

I blushed. "Ah, yes, you did."

"So how come you're here again?"

I stammered a bit. "Ah, well, I just went for a walk and needed to come back in again."

"Hmm, I must have missed seeing you slip back out of here."

I smiled weakly, collected my stuff, and left as quickly as possible. I had no idea what and how I'd ended up outside the airport, and had no desire to stick around and find out. As it was, I made it to my gate with only ten minutes to spare. They'd started the pre-boarding.

The flight to Melbourne was uneventful, although we were late leaving due to air congestion, which made me have to run like crazy to make my final flight. I had a tiny plane to my final destination, and as we rose and circled, I looked down from my window at the water below us. *Stacy, where on earth are you going to end up?*

The stewardess stopped beside me. "So where are you from?"

"Canada."

"And where are you going today?"

"I don't know."

She got a puzzled look. "Excuse me?"

"I flew into Sydney. A strange woman met me and handed me two tickets. This is the second ticket. Do you know where I'm going?"

Her eyebrows shot up. "I'm sorry; I'm just filling in for another stewardess. We'll be landing in Devonport, but I've never been here before." She cocked her head. "Do you honestly have no idea where you're going?"

I wistfully shook my head. "When God tells you to step out in faith, sometimes He really stretches that faith. Having come halfway around the world, I'm too far to turn back now."

When the plane landed in Devonport, I breathed a sigh of relief. It was a tiny airport with only a few people around. I walked across the tarmac from the airplane thinking this would be so easy …

Half an hour later when not a single soul was left and I was still sitting in the small corridor, I was nearly in tears again. It was 11:30 p.m. my time, and I had been flying for twenty-eight hours with basically no sleep and just adrenaline rushes to sustain me. I had no idea what to do. As I walked to the door, I saw a payphone. Suddenly I remembered the two-dollar coin Darla had given me. I'd been too busy to use it in Melbourne. As I approached the phone, I sent a prayer upward.

Lord, I have a coin for a phone—my only Australian money, since I haven't changed anything over. But now what?

What did the ladies tell you about a school?

They said Geneva, but what good does that do me?

Look in the phone book.

Under what? I don't know the name of the town where it's supposed to be located.

Just look.

When I picked up the phone book, my flagging courage bolstered. It was a thin book. By going through page after page, I came to an entry: Geneva Baptist School.

Oh, wow! Could this be it? Lord, I only have one coin. What if it's wrong?

Dial it.

I gulped and dialed with shaking hands.

After a couple of rings, a voice answered. "Geneva Baptist School. How may I help you?"

I hesitated.

"Hello? Is someone there?"

I stammered a bit. "Uh, yes, uhm ... look, this may sound really weird, but have you heard of a girl from Canada named Stacy Kanner?"

The voice became enthusiastic. "Oh, yes. She's planning to come and help in our school. Why? How do you know about that?"

"Because I'm her."

"Oh. Oh, so nice to talk to you. When are you coming?"

"I'm here."

"Here? Where, here?"

"I don't know." I started crying. I heard voices in the background, and then a man's voice joined the line.

"Hello. We are expecting a Stacy Kanner but weren't told when she'd arrive. Where did you say you were?"

I sniffled. "I don't know. I've landed at someplace called Devonport."

"Oh, that's just about a twenty-minute drive away. You just sit tight and don't go anywhere. We'll send someone over to pick you up right away."

The phone line clicked as I glared at it. "Don't go anywhere. Duh! Not likely."

The relief that I was going to be okay rushed over me as waves of exhaustion rolled in. Later I was to learn that the reason for such lack of planning was because the man bringing me over suddenly had a family crisis, so it was understandable that I would be forgotten in the turmoil he was experiencing.

By the time the car pulled up, my exhaustion had me seeing two heads on the man who came in for me.

As he hurried in, he exclaimed, "What a way to welcome you to Tasmania!" Naturally I started crying again. But by the time we pulled into the gum-tree-canopied lane to the school, I was under control again. I was given a whirlwind tour of the campus and then asked if I wanted to start teaching that afternoon. My eyes bugged out.

"I've been up and travelling for over thirty hours now; I just need to sleep." I stuttered my response and they looked surprised.

"But you've travelled before!" Their startled response made me realize they didn't understand what jet-lag did to me.

They kindly took me to the flat (apartment) I'd be sharing with three other single girls also working on campus. I dragged my weary body up the stairs and into the room they showed me and collapsed on the bed. It took a bit to wind down, then I knew nothing for hours until there was a knock on my door.

Chapter 27

I staggered to the door, feeling shell-shocked. When I opened it, the girl who would become my best friend in Australia stood there.

"Hi. I'm Abbie. I teach the youngest class here. We wondered if you'd like to come eat with us."

I blinked blearily. "Sure. Give me a couple minutes."

"Is there anything you're allergic to? I'm cooking tonight."

"I can't eat spicy food."

She stared at me puzzled. "I beg your pardon?"

"Spicy food is very hard for me."

She gave me a queer look and backed away from the door. It wasn't until much later that she said my accent confused her and she thought I didn't want spacey food, and she had no idea how Canadians cooked food with space.

Over the course of the meal, I learned that Camilla lived there permanently and had the grade five to six classroom. Melody was the school secretary, while Abbie was in her first year teaching there. They were there only during the weekdays and went home on the weekends. Our flat consisted of a small lounge and tiny kitchen. There was a two-burner stove with a tiny oven and a small fridge, but no sink. It was hard to wash up in a dish pan and carry the water from the bathroom each meal. When our sink finally arrived on September 14, we went out for fish and chips to celebrate. Shortly after the sink came in, the oven went out! We always seemed to have something happen in our home to keep our creative juices flowing on how to cook, clean, and keep the home afloat.

Each one of us was responsible to cook the evening meal once a week. Since I was the last to arrive, I was given Thursday evening. We each made our own breakfast and lunch, and on the weekends it was a "fend for yourself" deal.

There were three bedrooms close to the main bathroom, which held a sink, a toilet, and only a shower, not a tub. There was a tiny washing machine, but drying clothes was au' naturel. Hidden away at the end of a hall was a smaller room. They apologized for making me be in the back away from everyone, but when I opened up the door, I saw that the bedroom also contained an airplane-style restroom: a closet with a tiny toilet and sink. I was thrilled to have my own facilities alone in the back. I couldn't believe one of them hadn't wanted it.

The school itself was quite sprawled out. The campus was located in the country a bit away from the nearest town and nestled among 120 acres. Most of the married staff had houses on the land, and the one single guy had a small flat just below ours. It was a beautiful location with lots of space and animals. However, I hadn't come prepared for the Tasmania winter. You hear the word "Australia" and think "heat." So the majority of my clothes were planned for hot weather. Being surrounded by water, Tasmania had the most temperate climate of any of the six states and had a damp humidity to it. As a result, I was embarrassed to be a Canadian who was shivering in her unheated flat. Camilla finally found a small heater for me so I didn't have to spend all my evenings huddled in my bed. Another staff member kindly donated a coat for me until spring came along. On one trip into town, I found a cheap jumper (sweater) that I wore continuously.

There were 134 students attending Geneva Baptist School. Each class had its own little building, and all were connected to one another by a walkway with overhanging roofs. The only heat in the class came from a low tin pipe that ran across the top of the ceiling. There was a hole in one spot where the heat poured out. This happened to be over the scoring table, and I've never had a class that was more willing to score than this group. They were having a record cold winter, so I wasn't the only one shivering. After every single page, the students wanted to score so they could stand under the heat for as long as possible before returning to their cold, damp desks. At least we were on the tail end of winter when I arrived, so it wasn't too long before the heat wasn't needed.

I was assigned the grade two to four class, which consisted of twelve boys and two girls. The girls were fine, but the boys were very good at giving me a run for my money. I was replacing their teacher who was going on maternity leave, and she didn't have the energy to keep them under control. Thankfully a twelfth-grade student came every morning to help me, as I was swamped. Giselle was good with reading or anything else I wanted done. We got along well, although I wasn't sure to be insulted or not when she first met me.

"Ah, you're the new teacher. I'll help you an hour each morning. I'm working for a credit as a teacher's assistant."

I stuck out my hand. "I'm so thankful to see you. This is a very busy class."

She laughed. "These blokes can be right larrikins."

I stared at her blankly. She continued. "Don't let them intimidate you or they'll run over you."

I smiled as I realized she meant they were a handful. I'd already gathered that within the hour. By the time she was ready to leave, she had another comment.

"Oh, I'm right glad you came. I think you'll do just fine. We were worried when we heard the sheila coming was so old."

I stared at her again. She blithely went on. "But even as old as you are, you know how to keep up with these bludgers." She waved and walked out the door.

I shook my head. *Stacy, you need to buy an Australian dictionary or you're going to spend most of the time trying to interpret what people mean. And since when is twenty-six so old? Grrr!*

Another mum also volunteered to come in a couple times a week just to listen to the reading. That helped me. A lot of my time was needed to plan extra-curricular things beyond the Paces they worked on each morning. The sports and music were taught by someone else on Tuesday and Thursday, which were the classes I liked best. I was left with art, which I absolutely did not enjoy. I was extremely grateful when Abbie suggested we combine our classes for art each week. That gave us twenty-three students between the two teachers in the room, and it seemed to work better. She was also good at coming up with ideas, since that was not my forte. The swim class I did not have to teach; one of the mums was the swim coach, but I was expected to be in the pool and demonstrate all her instructions. This was a problem, as I am not a swimmer but a drowner.

My first time taking the class to the pool was a fiasco. When I realized I was supposed to get in the water, I tried to tell them I couldn't swim, but the lady was busy talking, so I reluctantly slid into the water.

How hard can this be, Stacy? You can touch bottom here and just help the students move about.

Next thing I knew the instructor had gathered the students and explained underwater breathing techniques to be able to glide the length of the pool underwater.

"Now your teacher will show you how it's done."

My head jerked up as I heard her say that. "What? No, I can't."

She waved her hand. "Go on, they're waiting for you."

"But ... I ... you never ... please."

She frowned at me. "Stop wasting our time. The children need every minute to practise. Now go!"

Here goes nothing, I thought as I took a deep breath and dropped below the water. As my ears filled with water, my sense of balance deteriorated and I started thrashing about, trying to decide which way was up. I opened my mouth and choked on water. Somewhere in the midst of my struggles, the head coach finally realized something was wrong and ordered her nine-year-old son, my student, to go rescue me. She gave the class a free swim time and came to me where I clutched the edge of the pool, gasping and sputtering.

"What happened?" Her eyes were concerned as she looked at me.

"I can't swim. I tried to tell you that."

Her eyes popped with shock. "But you're a teacher."

I gazed through bedraggled hair. "What has that to do with anything?"

"You have to have your swimming certification to be a teacher."

"Not where I'm from, you don't."

"Why not?" She looked genuinely puzzled.

I laughed. "Close to half of the year we walk on our water!"

"What?"

"Lady, most of our water is frozen a good portion of the year. We skate, sled, and ski on the lakes more than swim in them."

She apologized profusely for not listening to me and explained swimming was a basic part of schooling, since Tasmania was surrounded by water. She pointed to her two-year old who was swimming nearby with arm floats on. "I started all my children on swimming lessons when they were about six weeks old.

Now it was my turn to be astonished. "What? How can you even do that?"

"I use the bathtub and start with splashing water on their face. Next I dip them under the water bit by bit so they learn not to be afraid of water over their faces." She pointed to her daughter. "By the time they're two, I can drop them in the pool with floats and they go all over. She'll be ready to take them off when her legs strengthen a bit more."

I looked at her son, Damien. "He may struggle in the classroom, but here in the pool—"

"Yes," she interrupted. "He's a fish. I wonder if he'll go places."

"Go places?"

"I trained for the Olympics but didn't quite have what it takes. But in my son, I see more than what I had. So who knows?"

I was glad to hear that. When I see students struggle academically, it's so great to spot other areas in which they can excel. After all, classroom academics are only one phase of education. Life is full of education you can learn outside the classroom.

I learned to keep an eye on a few of the boys. Toby was the chatterbox. He had to be the first to tell anything and everything possible, and in high decibels. Blake wasn't noisy but so mischievous. I discovered his secret to know when he was planning something, which really annoyed him.

"Blake, whatever you're planning to do today, don't!"

"Miss Kanner, what do you mean?" He focused huge, innocent, baby blue eyes on me.

"The trick you're planning is not going to happen."

He scrunched up his nose. "Aww, you're no fun. How do you always know when I've got something planned?"

"I'm a teacher. Teachers know things!" I waggled my eyebrows at him, and he grinned as he walked away.

Even Giselle asked me about it. "Miss Kanner, every time Blake has a scheme, you know about it before he does it. How do you figure it out?"

I laughed. "You know how people have habits?"

"Yes."

"Well, I've noticed that every time he plans a trick, he gives me a gift the day before."

"Really? How did you notice that?"

"He brought me daffodils the day before he tied the girls into the restroom. He gave me a scrunchie for my hair the day before he stuck the water bucket on top of the slightly opened door. So now when I get a gift, I'm ready for something to happen the next day."

Giselle laughed and laughed. "Wow! Do you think he's saying sorry before the stunt instead of after it?"

I shrugged. "Whatever it is, it's a great pointer for me, so don't you dare tell him how I know when he's planning stuff."

Arthur always liked to pull a disappearing act to see how long it would take to find him. I solved that problem accidentally. The property had some excellent climbing trees, which were off limits for the students. A few years earlier someone had fallen out of one and broken an arm. But trying to keep nine-year-old boys out of them was hard. With the spring came multiple leaves and good screening from the eyes of the teacher on duty. So the boys would still sneak out and climb them.

The students had gone outside for break. I was rummaging through a cupboard and came across a boomerang.

Oh, wow! A boomerang. The first real one I've ever seen! I've got to go and see if it'll come back to me.

I hustled out of the class and looked around. I didn't want anyone to spot me, so I went to the edge of the boundary and flung back my arm. "Whoo-eeeee!" I shrieked as I hurtled it as high and as far as I could go. With my dreadful aim, instead of circling gracefully, it flew straight into the big old oak tree. I heard a yelp and a thump as a boy dropped out of the tree.

"Crikey! Don't hit us again. We'll get out!" Two more boys dropped down and trudged over to me. I stared at Arthur, Toby, and Blake. Toby, of course, had to be the spokesman.

"Miss Kanner, fair dinkum! How did you know we were up there? We've been hiding in it all week, and not one teacher ever found us."

Blake rolled his eyes. "Strewth, mate. This teacher knows everything. I'll sure be glad when she goes back to Canada. We can't do nuttin' around here anymore."

I struggled not to laugh as Arthur added his two cents' worth. "But hitting us with our own boomerang? That's no fair go! The other teacher took it away from us when she caught us knocking down the bird feeders with it just before you got here."

I tried to look stern. "Consider it poetic justice." They looked puzzled but resigned as I sent them to wash down the walkway as punishment for being out of bounds and up in the tree. I nearly jumped out of my skin when a voice sounded over my shoulder.

"Did you really know those boys were in that tree? I can't see you deliberately trying to hit them." Slade Canmore had a knowing look in his eye as he walked over and plucked my boomerang out of the tree.

I blushed. "How much did you see?"

He grinned. "All of it. I was coming to look for those boys." He paused. "I think you're good for them. They've had gentle teachers up until now."

I frowned. "Am I to be insulted or complimented?"

"You have a lot of energy. You know how to keep them on their toes, and I think they respect you for it."

"They sure didn't sound like it right now."

He laughed. "No self-respecting bloke is going to want to admit he got knocked out of a tree by a sheila with a boomerang—especially when you don't have a clue how to throw it properly."

I rolled my eyes, but he was right. Although he showed me several times, I could not get that thing to sail back to me like he could.

Not only did the boys give me a challenge, but so did the Australian animals.

Chapter 28

I knew Australia had some interesting animals, but I didn't realize the Tasmanian devil was real and not just a cartoon character. Abbie filled me in on that when I came in after dark one night.

"Abbie, when I crossed the yard, I saw some eyes staring at me. What kind of animals do we have around here?"

She looked up from her book. "Oh, I never thought to tell you to be careful. Most of the animals won't hurt you, except the Tasmanian devil."

I snorted. "Yeah, right."

"Seriously. The Tasmanian tiger is considered to be extinct, but the devil is a smallish animal that you don't want to mess with."

"Why?"

"Its jaws have the third most powerful pinching power of any animal. It can crush bones and bite through thick metal wire. They can climb trees, swim rivers, and run quickly for short periods of time."

I stared at her. "And no one thought to tell me about this?"

She shrugged. "They're nocturnal animals, so we rarely see them. But one has been sighted around here, so if you're out at night, keep a watch out for eyes glowing in the dark."

I groaned. "Oh, thanks. Way to wreck my going out at night to gaze at your Southern Cross and other stars."

She giggled. "I don't think he'll be aggressive to you if he doesn't feel threatened. I've never had any trouble here in the evenings."

Nevertheless, I felt more on edge walking across the compound at night after that. When I mentioned it to the Canmores, they took me to a wildlife preserve, where a ranger gave a talk in the devil's den. The mama devil became impatient for her food and suddenly leapt at the ranger. She jumped out of the way, but the devil caught the back of her steel-toed work boot and simply tore it off like a strip of crust from bread. The ranger tossed her a dead rabbit to distract her; I could hear her grinding all the bones as she ate it.

Slade and Jasmine also assured me that most of the nighttime eyes peering at me were harmless nocturnal animals, but I stayed cautious. The opossums were ugly but harmless, the wallabies (small kangaroos) left you alone, the wombats wouldn't hurt you, while the platypus was extremely difficult to find, as they were shy creatures and I just caught a glimpse now and then as they slipped into the water. But the devil was vicious. Thankfully I never had a run-in with one.

I got to hold a wombat at a wildlife park and was surprised at the weight. They feel a bit like a soft teddy bear and are a puff of air to pick up around the body. But their rear end is hard bone, and that's where their weight of fifty to seventy-seven pounds comes from. It's their defence mechanism. They burrow their top body into the ground and let the attacker hit their rear end. It can crush the skull of foxes, dogs, and other animals. I was warned never to hit the end of a wombat or it would wreck the front end of the ute (pickup).

The wallabies were a main part of life down under as food and in conversation. I was driving with Abbie and she accidentally popped the clutch.

She looked at me and laughed. "Guess I filled up the tank with 'roo juice."

I looked blank. "Huh?"

"Roo juice. You know how kangaroos jump—"

"Actually, I don't. I haven't seen one yet."

"Well, they are massive jumpers. So if you jerk your car at all, we joke that instead of gas, we've filled with 'roo juice."

"Oh, I get it." I laughed and she gazed at me sympathetically. I had much to learn culturally. I was never sure if the older students were pulling my leg or not, as they got a kick out of indoctrinating me into Aussie ways.

One evening a group of us went to McDonalds. I looked at my wrapper and laughed. "Hey, this states this burger is 100% Australian beef."

One guy nudged me. "Know what that means?"

"No, what?"

"You're eating 'roo meat."

I looked at my meat. "Really?"

They laughed, so I wasn't sure. They did shoot wallaby for meat, just as some Canadians do with moose or deer. The first time I ate 'roo meat was a wallaby stew.

My hostess watched me. "So what do you think of 'roo meat?"

I chewed carefully and swallowed. "Good, but it's bouncy."

They laughed and laughed, but I wasn't joking. As I chewed it seemed my teeth went "ka-boing" more than with other meat. I thought maybe it was because the majority of the kangaroo meat was in their powerful leg muscles.

Wallabies are a smaller kangaroo member and usually grow to a height of three to six feet compared to the mainlanders, which often grow to eight feet. As such, wallabies also jump only about six feet high, whereas the bigger relatives can have a jump as high as ten feet. But I was thoroughly impressed with even the smaller ones' range of jump. I came around the corner of a house one day and found myself eyeball to eyeball with a wallaby.

"*A-a-a—h-h!*" I let out a screech of surprise, which scared the 'roo breathing in my face. His ears twitched and—k-a-b-o-i-n-g! The thing went from flat-footed to over my head and bounded away as I stared in shock. At five-foot-three-inches, I'm not the world's tallest person, but for a 'roo to just sail over my head was astonishing.

"Hey!" I yelled after it. "Come back here and do that again!" Of course, it ignored me.

The other animal that gave me a shock was the kookaburra. Since we didn't have a clothes dryer, we hung everything on the line to dry. The first week I was there I stood at the line hanging my clothes. Suddenly from nowhere this crazed "ahhhaaaakkkueeerrrrra" laugh sounded. I dropped my clothespins in fright. Looking around I saw no one. I shakily picked up the next shirt and started to pin it. Insane laughter rippled out. I called out, "Hello? Anyone here?" More insane laughter. I lost my nerve, dropped the clothes, and ran for the buildings. Partway there I met Slade Canmore.

He took a look at my face. "Stacy, what's wrong?"

I puffed to a halt. "Does Latrobe have a mental institution?"

He chuckled. "No, of course not. It's way too small. Why?"

"Because I think some inmate has escaped from somewhere. There's a crazy person down by the clothesline."

Slade craned his neck. "I don't see anyone out there."

"No, that's the problem." I pressed my hand against my heart. "But someone is hiding somewhere and laughed insanely when I tried to find them."

Slade threw back his head and laughed and then tried to sober up when I glared at him. "Sorry, Stacy, you're just so funny. Did you by any chance see a brown bird with a white head sitting on a fence post?"

I frowned. "Of course not; I was looking for a person, not a bird."

He patted my shoulder. "The kookaburra has a variety of calls that sound like humans laughing. Its loudest, aggressive one can sound like a crazy person. You'll get used to their calls."

I shivered. "I don't think I want to get used to that one!" I went back to my laundry and, sure enough, spied the bird Slade had told me about. I'm not sure I ever grew accustomed to the eeriest call it made. We had quite a few of those birds there, and the gentle calls were actually fun. I'm convinced one certain bird hated me and took great delight in making that horror laugh that set my teeth on edge whenever it saw me.

The koala was not native to Tasmania, so I never saw one until I went to the mainland with the Canmores. They took me to a wildlife preserve. Soon Slade motioned me to come over to him. He was standing with a koala. "Would you like to hold this little guy?"

"Man, he's cute. Sure." He transferred him to my arms, and the little guy clutched at my arm. "Phew!"

Slade grinned. "What's wrong? Don't like the aroma?"

"He sure stinks. I think he's a lot cuter from a distance! These claws are sharp, too." I was glad to hold it to say that I had, but then was equally glad to let it go. My sense of smell is quite acute, and I was trying not to gag from the odour emanating from that little guy.

I did not like the emus. At the wildlife entrance you could buy an ice cream cone filled with seeds to feed the animals. I was walking along holding my cone when an aggressive emu came up and stared me in the eyes. "Give me that cone," is what I interpreted his squawk to mean.

"Get lost," I muttered. "This is my cone, and it's for the nice animals."

Quick as a wink that nasty thing gave me the evil eye, thrust out its beak, and snatched the cone out of my hand.

"Hey!" I yelled and made a grab for it. He danced out of the way, and all I was left with was a feather in my hand. Everyone with me thought it was hilarious, while I was just mad. But I wasn't about to tackle him to retrieve my food supply, as they have powerful beaks, and he was as tall as I was.

As we left the park several hours later, Jasmine asked, "So what did you think?"

"The echidna (anteater) reminded me of our porcupines, and the other animals were interesting. But I guess I'm not a bird person. I'm still mad at that emu, and the cockatoo was so annoying. It called me names!"

Slade laughed. "You don't have good taste, I see."

"Huh? What's that got to do with anything?"

"Both birds are very valuable. Each can be well over $1,000.00."

My jaw dropped. "You're kidding?"

"Nope. The cockatoo is protected as well, since outside of Australia they can be considered an endangered species."

"Well, both of them are going to be 'in danger' if they don't leave me alone," I muttered as I saw that emu coming toward me again. The Canmores just laughed.

Although I saw these animals at natural wildlife parks, the majority of them I also saw periodically in nature, since we lived in the country. I loved watching certain ones, while others made me extremely cautious.

Chapter 29

Although the reason I'd gone to Australia was to teach, naturally one wants to get as much sightseeing in as possible. The people there were wonderful about inviting me to go places with them. Tasmania is an amazing place to visit. Although it was cold until November, I was so thankful for the moderate climate. Once I went to the mainland, I longed for the easier weather of Tasmania. However, rain and grey were as common as the sun and beauty, so you had to take the elements as they came.

One of the volunteer mums, Aimee Burns, came to me one day.

"We have a caravan and are taking a weekend trip. There's an extra bunk in it if you want to come along."

Of course, I happily accepted and had the privilege of going to the West Coast with the Burns. We went by Cradle Mountain. It's one of the most well-known mountains but has a reputation of having only a few days where the sun shines all day. So if you want to hike it, plan on being very wet, as you will have mist, fog, drizzle, and full-blown downpours in the course of the day. That also makes it difficult to fully see the top of the two peaks, which creates the "cradle" effect. We didn't stop to hike, but it was nice to see at least the part not shrouded in clouds.

We went to Zeehan, and I loved the ride, although I was glad I wasn't driving since there's barely any straight stretches of road in that area. There are so many mining towns and ghost towns because of mining in the West Coast. I spent some time browsing the very good museum in Zeehan. One interesting moment occurred at a rock display as I spied a certain rock.

"Wow, isn't that a pretty rock?" At my exclamation, Aimee hurried over to look, read the inscription, and then started to laugh. "What's so funny?" I asked.

"Did you look at the label?"

"No." I came over to see what she saw and had to laugh, too. "I guess I know quality when I see it!" The rock had been brought over from Canada and donated to the display.

Since they had friends in the area, we parked in their yard for the night. Their son, Cliff, offered me an extremely interesting evening.

"Ya' be a sheila that handles bushwalkin'?" He didn't talk a lot, so afterward his mum told me she was surprised he even offered.

"I grew up on a farm."

"I'm headed on a wallaby hunt, if'n ya want ta' come." He headed for the door. I looked at Aimee for permission, and when she nodded, I quickly grabbed my jacket and followed. We went to his ATV and headed up the mountain for at least an hour. The tracks (roads) he took me on wound up and over and into places I wasn't sure we'd make it through.

"Look up ahead." He nudged my shoulder. We saw four wallabies hopping along.

"Oh, they're so cute." I looked at him. I was a farm gal so knew butchering was a part of life. "Do you have to shoot these ones?"

"Na. I got a good meat supply earlier this month. Figured ya'd just want to shoot with a camera on this trip." He grinned at me.

I smiled back. "Yeah. I'm sure to you it's like us shooting our yearly steer for meat, but I'm glad I can just enjoy watching these little creatures."

From the top of the mountain, we could look down at the town of Zeehan. He was surprisingly patient with me as I oohed and aahed about things. Finally he drove me through the Spray Tunnel. That was an experience! It's an abandoned train tunnel that was carved through the hill to move ore from the silver mine. It was one hundred metres long, and the headlights picked up some glow worms hanging from the ceiling. It was creepy and scary and crazy and amazing all at the same time. It was so narrow that I thought we might get stuck, and that made me rather claustrophobic. I was glad when we made it through but didn't regret having experienced it.

The next day we continued to Queenstown. Aimee tossed a question at me over her shoulder. "Do you get carsick?"

I turned my gaze from the window in the back seat. "No. Why?"

"Good. We want to take you on the Ninety-Nine Bends."

"What's that?"

"It's part of the Lyell Highway and is famous for having ninety-nine bends in three-and-a-half miles. Although it's not quite that many anymore, as they've straightened some of the road."

As we twisted and turned, I could understand why she asked that question. "You certainly don't want to take anyone that gets carsick on this road. But it's so neat to see the layers of road twisting like a snake down under us. I think I counted five roads below."

"We thought you'd find this interesting."

I have to admit that when we stopped to get out and look around, I did feel a little lightheaded.

Another couple invited me over for a special dining event. I was glad it was on a Friday, as the supper lasted from 6:30 p.m. until midnight. They had a chef friend who planned a seven-course meal for us. I'd never had such a thing before, and at the first course I thought, *Sheesh, Stacy, you're going to starve here. Such a tiny portion.* By the fourth course I thought, *Sheesh, Stacy, you needed a looser skirt.* By the seventh course I thought, *Sheesh, Stacy, it hurts to move!* The food was amazing, but the number of dishes even more so. The chef insisted on a different plate, fork, et cetera for each of the courses. It was neat to experience, but I'm glad I need to wash dishes for only one meal when I cook, and that it doesn't take five hours to eat it. We had a type of fried cracker for the hors d'oeuvre and a light soup for the entrée. The third course was a lemon chicken followed by a veggie dish with pork. Next came noodles and beef, and lamb ribs was the last of the meat. Our final course was an apple crumble dessert. It was so kind of them to include me in this special meal when they didn't know me that well.

Another couple, Jordan and Maggie Horne, took me under their wing. Their sons were no longer in school, but they still supported the staff there. I had many fun times in their beautiful home. One entire outer wall was glass, as the house overlooked the Bass Strait, and you could watch all the activity on the waves.

When she took me to her garden, I just closed my eyes and hummed. She looked at me. "Is something wrong?"

I opened my eyes. "I feel like I've died and gone to heaven."

"Of course you haven't. It's just a garden." But I could tell by her little smile that she was pleased with my response.

"You have the most gorgeous smells out here."

"That's the aromas of the wisteria and jasmine. They are lovely, aren't they?"

I took a deep breath of the scent wafting over me. "Look at the riotous colours rippling across the yard from all your flowers and bushes. This is like walking into a bunch of floral shops and greenhouses all combined into one back yard. Unbelievable!"

She smiled. "I like working with flowers. It's fun trying to arrange the plants so the colours make it look like a patchwork quilt out here."

At supper that night, Jordan spoke to me. "I know it's a bit far to walk to Latrobe easily, so we wondered if you like to bike?"

"I love it. I have one at home I use all the time."

"We'd be glad to let you use our oldest son's bicycle. He's in college so isn't using it right now."

"If he doesn't mind, I'd be grateful. Then I can get into town without needing to beg a ride from someone. I hate having to do that."

Jordan laughed. "I'd noticed your independence. That's why I offered. I'll bring it in the ute the next time I stop at school."

The Hornes invited me along on a weekend trip with them to Hobart. One stop was to see the Cat and Fiddle Square. It was built in 1962 and featured the nursery rhyme. On the hour the cat played the fiddle, the cow sailed over the moon, and the dish and spoon peeped out from behind the clock. I loved seeing that so much, I made sure I came back at the next hour to watch it again.

The couple the Hornes and I stayed with while in Hobart had been to Manitoba. He was a retired science professor who had been invited to lecture at the U of M in Winnipeg. I felt like I'd met family when they knew the places I talked about. Since his area of expertise was bees, they gave me two small tins of honey when I left—Blue Gum and Leatherwood. It was very different from the honey I was used to in Manitoba.

Slade and Jasmine Canmore were a couple I became quite close to while in Tasmania. They'd been there only two years so understood some of my loneliness, even though they came from the mainland. They didn't have the culture shock to deal with, but had also lived in the United States once, so they knew the feeling of leaving family and friends to move to the unknown. It took sixteen days for a letter to reach me, and while I could call home much easier than in Peru, it was too expensive to do it more than once or twice. Slade reminded me of my brother, Jason. I often went to him when things seemed too much. He was the volleyball coach and sometimes asked me to fill in on practices if someone was missing. Jasmine became a good friend. She was an excellent cook and taught me many of their Aussie recipes. Their two little boys were well-behaved, and I found myself invited many times for tea and games around their table. I loved the game "Squatter." It was Monopoly with an Aussie twist, as you bought and sold sheep for your station. I looked everywhere for it and finally managed to buy one as my Aussie souvenir.

Even Giselle Mayer, my young helper each morning, invited me a few times to her place.

"Miss Kanner, our family wants to go on a bushwalk this weekend. Would you like to come home with me on Friday and join us?"

"Ooh, I'd love that. Let me get my map." Whenever I went somewhere, I'd get people to show me where we were going.

"We want to trek around Explorer Lake. It'll be an all-day deal, as it'll take close to two hours to get there."

So I had a lovely tea with them Friday evening with singing around the piano. We hiked to Explorer Lake on Saturday and had a barbecue in the bush out there. Tasmanians were so good with making small campfires and slapping on a couple of burgers to eat. You do have to be prepared for any weather, though, as it can be sunny, then rainy, then sunny. One day in school I counted seven times the rain just bucketed down. But in between it was beautiful weather.

I also learned that when you asked for a hamburger, that's what you got—two pieces of bread with a hamburger in between them. But if you asked for a hamburger sandwich, you had the meat, then a slice of each: onion, beetroot (picked beet), pineapple, tomato, and topped with a leaf of lettuce. I was skeptical of the combination, so it was good that I was eating it at night and couldn't see it the first time I tried it. The explosion of taste was different, but I decided I liked it.

Chapter 30

Besides being my roommate, Abbie became a best friend to me. She always went home for the weekend, and many times she invited me along. She lived over in Somerset, which was only about an hour away. She was an intrepid hiker and had no fear of driving anywhere in Tasmania, so I really got to explore with her. Distance was not an issue, as Tasmania is roughly only four hours drive north to south or east to west. For me, coming from a country that is nearly five thousand kilometres from east to west, any drive in Tasmania seemed like nothing.

"Hey, Stacy, how about a bushwalk?" Abbie came into my room a week or so after my arrival.

"What's that?" I looked up from my papers I was grading.

"Uhm, how do you Americans say it—take a hike?" She grinned.

"Oh, yes, I'd love to. Where were you thinking?"

"My brother just challenged me to see if I could beat his time through The Gorge. There's a nice picnic area at the bottom. We could tramp along in there and take a packed lunch tomorrow if you like."

"Aren't you going home?"

"Not this weekend. I have too many papers." Abbie pointed at my pile. "Just like you do. How about a break? Let's do some music."

I scrambled to my feet. "Sounds like a great plan." Not only did we both like the outdoors, but we shared a love of music. Over the period of time I was there, we held numerous "fun" sessions. I joined her in a quartet for their church music for special events, and we were often asked to bring our guitar, keyboard, flute, et cetera along on youth events. To be out on the beach in the glow of the moon singing around a campfire with her were some of my best memories.

We left early the next morning. The Gorge was eleven kilometres of extremely winding road all the way down to the bottom and back up the other side. We ran through it but were three minutes behind his time. I looked at Abbie.

"Are you sure he gave you the right time? If we go any faster on those curves, we'll overshoot and land in the gorge!"

She rubbed her neck where the seatbelt had left a mark. "Maybe if we try it from this side, we'll get a better time. How ya' going?"

I grinned. "Let's do it."

She reached for the stick. "Goodonya. Got the time?"

I reached for my watch. "Ready, set, go." We tore off and started in on the curves. When we got to the top, I looked at the watch. "Well, this way is better. We shaved two minutes off, but he's still beating us by one minute."

She looked at me. "Wanna give it one more go?"

I was feeling slightly dizzy but shrugged. "Sure, why not?"

After the third try, we admitted he could outrace us on that crazy road and settled down to have a good time trekking through the bottom area.

One weekend we couldn't leave for her place until late Friday evening due to an event at school. So it was fairly dark as we drove along the north shore. Suddenly from the corner of my eye, I saw movement.

"Say, what is that?" I pointed and then gasped when Abbie abruptly pulled over and stopped. "Did I say something wrong?"

She turned and grinned. "No! But even I don't see these often. They're fairy penguins."

At first I thought she was pulling my leg. "Yeah, right. Even I know penguins are black, not blue like these things."

Abbie shook her head and continued. "Fairy penguins are slate-blue and only live about six years. They don't grow more than a foot tall. Since they're so different, I guess that's why they're called fairies. They're only found in Australia and New Zealand, and not many people get to see them in the natural like this. Shh, don't slam the door and let's see if we can get close."

We slid out of the car and slowly moved toward the flock of little things waddling about. The hiss, squeals, and growls they were making masked us until we were right among them. Suddenly I heard barking, and with a flutter of wings the entire group went waddling over the cliff and disappeared into the night. I looked around. "Say, where's the dog?"

Abbie laughed. "That was one of the male fairies. They can make all kinds of different sounds. Guess he was telling them we were intruders and to vamoose. That was fun. I don't think I've ever gotten that close to them before."

Another weekend we headed to Dip Falls. Since it was an all-day jaunt, we decided to buy some pasties for our lunch. Abbie pulled up next to the shop selling them in her light beige vehicle. "I'll just wait if you want to jump out and get them for us."

"Sure, no problem," I said and grabbed my purse. Running into the store, I quickly made my purchases and dashed out. I jumped into my seat and buckled up.

"All right, let's go!" I chanted. "I'm ready for some fun."

To my horror, a deep male voice responded with amusement. "Your wish is my command, lady. Where should we go first?"

I whipped my head around and found myself staring into the face of a strange man.

He laughed. "I'll gladly spend the day with you."

I frantically looked behind me and spied Abbie in her beige car, which was parked just behind this stranger's beige car. Her head was leaning against the side window, and I could see she was laughing like a hyena.

My face went bright red, and I stuttered and stammered as I helplessly tried to unbuckle myself. "I am *so* sorry, sir! I got the wrong beige car."

He laughed again as he leaned over to unbuckle me, since I was making such a muddle of it. "Ah, even better, a foreigner by the sound of your voice. Sure I can't persuade you to chuck the bloke you planned to go with somewhere?"

"She's not a bloke; she's my best friend here—at least she was until now!" I managed to extricate myself from his vehicle. "Again, I'm sorry. I'm not good with recognizing vehicles."

He grinned. "Good thing I wasn't driving a paddy wagon."

I frowned. "A what?"

"The van that takes prisoners to jail." He laughed at my expression. "Go on with ya, mate. Have a good day." I slammed his door, and he waved and drove off. I stomped back to Abbie's car and pulled the door open.

"Thanks so much for your help. Sitting here laughing while I make a fool of myself!" I huffed as I buckled in once again.

She gasped for breath. "I tried. I truly did. I honked and everything, but you were enamored with getting in with that guy and totally ignored me." She grinned. "I don't blame you; he was very cute—or didn't you notice that, either?"

"No! I didn't. I was too embarrassed."

She put the car into gear. "Well, I'll have to keep an eye on you. Wouldn't want you to walk over the falls accidentally because you missed seeing it."

"Ha, ha. You're so funny."

Dip Falls was a beautiful place. I found all of the hiking in Tasmania was gorgeous. The manferns grew taller than I was and gave beautiful shade as you hiked amongst the forests there. We had 155 steps to get down to the bottom. The falls had a couple distinct dips to them, hence the name. Of course, what goes down, must come up. It was nice to have a whole day to leisurely explore the area.

We ate our pasties sitting on a log. When we finished, Abbie said, "We need to see 'The Big Tree' while we're here."

"What's that?"

"One of the largest trees in the southern hemisphere. It's our eucalyptus tree and about sixty-five metres high."

When we got there, it took us thirty-six giant steps to walk around it. By helping each other, we managed to boost ourselves up onto the root (higher than our head) to take photos of each other.

I threw out my arms as Abbie took my photo. "Me and the biggest tree ever!"

She lowered the camera. "Actually, it isn't quite as high as 'The Centurion.' That's the largest known eucalyptus and is also in Tasmania. It's almost one hundred metres high."

I shook my head and slid down from the root. "The constant rain and sun must be why you have such massive trees. The redwoods in northern California are the only other massive trees I know. And that climate has a lot of mist and fog and rain, too. Thankfully it doesn't have the same effect on people. I've had enough mist on me here to be about ten feet tall by now."

When we were back in the car, Abbie turned to me. "Do you have enough energy to go somewhere else?"

"You're the driver. Where you lead, I follow." She snickered. "What?" I questioned.

She put on a mock-serious face. "Only when you aren't distracted by some guy in another vehicle."

I punched her lightly in the arm. "You aren't going to let me forget about that, are you?"

"Stacy, I'm driving a Toyota Corona. That was a totally different make and model."

I rolled my eyes. "You have a beige car. He had a beige car. You have four wheels and a steering wheel. He had four wheels and a steering wheel. What's the difference?"

Now it was her turn to roll her eyes. "Never tell that to my brother. A mechanic would have a fit over that comment!" She put the car into motion.

"Where are we going now?"

"The Nut."

"The Nut? What kind of a nutty name is that?"

She smiled. "Oh, you'll see when we get to it." That's all she would say.

As we drove across some level ground and I looked out into the distance, I suddenly realized what she meant.

"Oh, wow, that does look like a big ol' hazelnut just sticking up in the middle of nowhere!" I looked at Abbie. "What is it?"

"They say it's a volcanic plug." At my puzzled look, she continued. "It's 143 metres above sea level, and people believe it came from an active volcano tons of years ago."

"That's so weird just sitting out there all by its lonesome. Are people allowed to try and go up it?"

"You bet. There's a pretty steep slope, but you get to see neat stuff on the way up. If you can't hike it, there's a chairlift you can pay to use."

"What should we do?"

Abbie looked at me. "I think it's best to hike up. It'll take us about an hour, but we can stop and take photos. Then let's take the chairlift going down. The view as you descend is phenomenal."

So that's what we did, and she was right. It was a hard climb but so worth the effort. By going down in the chairlift instead of up, we had a panoramic view of the strait and the nearby town of Stanley.

When we had several days off due to a school break, Abbie chose to venture further afield. We used the days to explore down in the Hobart area. Hobart, the capital, was Tasmania's largest city with a population of about 160,000. Abbie had friends in the area we could stay with for the nights. She wanted to tour a college that was there, so we had a fun day there after driving down via the midlands.

The next day she looked at me. "You like chocolate, right?"

I laughed. "Do fish swim? Do elephants have long noses? Of course. Why?"

"How'd you like to take the Cadbury Cruise?"

"What's that?"

She laughed. "It's advertised as 'the sweetest cruise in all of Australia' because we end up at the Cadbury Chocolate Factory."

"Ooh, sweet!"

"Exactly."

"No, I mean, cool. I've only been to the Hershey Chocolate Factory in Pennsylvania. This will be great."

We bought our tickets and boarded the boat for our two-hour cruise. Although the chocolate factory was the main part of the tour, we saw many other interesting things, too. We went under the Tasman Bridge, which wasn't quite as long as the Mackinac Bridge in Michigan, but very impressive. We saw the main gasworks for Tasmania and then spent a bit of time listening and looking at the catamaran works. I knew nothing about catamarans, so I was intrigued.

"If these wave-piercing boats are so fast compared to normal ones, why isn't everyone using them?"

Abbie smirked at my ignorance. "Yes, we could get to the mainland in four hours instead of overnight on the regular boat, but you're forgetting something."

"What?"

"Most boats ride the waves, which is a lulling motion. These catamarans cut through the waves so take an awful pounding. Ninety-eight per cent of the passengers spend their four hours barfing instead of enjoying an evening eating, sleeping, and watching the ocean like on the regular ship. Which would you prefer doing?"

"Oh." That ended that discussion.

We had a two-hour tour of the chocolate factory. Although I loved going through and sampling all their varieties, at the end I turned to Abbie.

"I don't think I'd want to work here."

"Why not? You get all the broken stuff to eat that you want."

"The smell is getting to me. It's just—too sweet. It's also a lot hotter and noisier in here than I expected."

Abbie said, "I agree. But I have to buy some chocolate here or my nephew and niece won't forgive me."

When we got to the shop at the end of the tour, we went halves on a five kg (eleven pound) box of chocolate for $25.00. "Wow! I didn't know they even made boxes this big!" I staggered in exaggeration when I first picked it up.

"I'm not sure if they sell such large boxes to regular stores, but this is where people come who want to buy bulk." Abbie added as we walked off. "I'm glad we went together to buy this one. It's much cheaper to buy bulk."

Back at the dock we had a bit of spare time before the boat returned for us. There were souvenir shops along the wharf, so I went searching. I was delighted to come across some outback Aussie hats.

"Abbie, look! How cool! Why do they have all these little corks hanging from string around the brim like this?"

"The outback has such massive numbers of insects and mosquitoes that they created these hats to help keep them away from your face. As you work, the strings and corks keep swaying, just like you brushing your hand in front of your face. That way you can still work with your hands instead of swatting flies all the time."

"I've got to buy a couple of these. That is totally neat. I need to try to implement these back in Manitoba. We have horrible mosquitoes in the summer." I bought one for myself and my sister-in-law, as well as a few other things before returning to the dock.

Everything was so unique and wonderful I couldn't help saying "this is the best" on each event. Abbie just kept laughing. But as a history fan, the day she took me to Port Arthur truly was a remarkable day for me. The history there is phenomenal.

"I'd already known a lot about Australia starting as a penal colony for Britain. I didn't know Tasmania had colonies here, too."

Abbie sighed. "Port Arthur was known for the severe cruelty inflicted there. Some of the convicts sent over weren't desperate criminals, just desperate people trying to survive in the terrible living conditions back in the late 1800s."

"Why is Port Arthur so special?"

"It was the most secure penal colony because it's almost an island in itself. The only way on and off is through Eaglehawk Neck. See that strip we're going to drive on?" Abbie gestured to a narrow stretch of land in front of us. "This is only thirty metres wide. They tied vicious dogs on long chains to posts sunk into the middle of the causeway. That closed up any access off that way. They didn't have to worry about guarding the rest of the island very much, as there are two-hundred-foot drops down these steep cliffs. Not many men tried to escape that way, either."

As we drove along the route, Abbie told me some of the stories. "Nobody escapes from Port Arthur. Between the cliffs, the dogs, and the vicious punishment for attempting, very few even tried it. There were just three that actually made it. The fourth guy would have, but he outsmarted himself."

I looked at her curiously. "How's that?"

She grinned at me. "He was an actor. Actors are strange people."

Since she knew I was into acting, I just rolled my eyes. "Go on."

"He managed to kill a kangaroo out in the bush one day. After skinning it, he sewed himself into it and hopped across this causeway we're on."

I laughed. "That's not strange. That's smart. Why didn't he make it?"

"Because the guards were so hungry, when they saw the 'roo, they grabbed their guns to shoot it for meat. When they heard the kangaroo say as he hopped by, 'Don't shoot me, don't shoot me,' they figured something was up!"

We both laughed. As we parked and got out of the car, shivers went down my spine. It was a beautiful day, and I was standing in the middle of history. "Some of this stonework is incredible!"

Abbie nodded. "The men were worked to death to build this place. They didn't believe in using anything other than manual labour. No horses were allowed to help haul the stone and rock. Men had to carry it all by hand. They had a sawmill here. Seventy men would carry the log to the mill. If someone fell and died, they just sent another man to take his spot."

"So much misery and spite here, wasn't there?" I looked around. "There's a huge difference between the area for the officers' quarters and the area for the prisoners." We headed off to tour the grounds. I went into one of the punishment cells for ten seconds and had to get out. "That's terrible."

Abbie nodded. "You wouldn't think just a cold, damp, stone black, dead silent little cubicle could affect you like that. But they say it took only four days for a man to go insane in there."

"I was so disoriented when you shut that door. I didn't know what was up or down. I can't imagine staying in there. You didn't even open it fast enough for me."

"A lot of men were stuck in here for anywhere up to a month. Besides being insane, they were usually blind and deaf when they came out."

"It's horrible." I shivered.

"This was the first time they experimented with psychological punishment instead of brutal physical labour. They also had a system of rewards as well as punishment, so not everyone was treated horribly."

"I guess it depended on whether or not you got on a guard's bad side, eh?"

Abbie agreed and we headed into the Separate Prison. To our delight, a twenty-man band from Adelaide was setting up in the centre. I plopped myself down on the cold, hard slab of concrete. "This is so awesome!"

Abbie dropped beside me. "I never knew this was here today."

For forty-five minutes we listened to a concert that swelled and swirled about us in the amazing acoustics of that stone jail painstakingly made by the convicts of two centuries ago. As they finished with their final number, "Amazing Grace," shivers rolled over me. "I will never forget this moment," I whispered to Abbie. From her nod, I could see she agreed.

We went into the chapel and I choked. "No, not really?"

Abbie laughed. "I couldn't wait to watch you see this. Chapel was mandatory, and the preacher was assured of each prisoner's undivided attention. Shall I take your photo?" She moved to the lectern while I stepped into the row that was built for my approximate height. I lifted the bar and stuck my neck into the yoke and shut the side doors on either side of me. "Did they really have to stand like this for the entire sermon?"

"Yup." Abbie snapped away. "You couldn't see or talk to anyone that way, and your head was focused directly at the preacher."

"Whew!" I called out. "Sure hope they didn't have long-winded preachers back then!" I changed places to take Abbie's photo. Since she was taller than I, she went back one row to a bit higher stand. "Each row is a few inches taller than the previous one, so you were sent in according to your height to take your place for the sermon."

"Wow. This is quite the place."

"Yeah, they shut down in 1877, and for a while they were going to demolish this place, as the cruelty here was an embarrassment to society, but then the historical societies started to realize the value of it. Now it's becoming a major tourist attraction."

It took us about four hours to finish our walk around the place.

When we returned to the car and had our lunch, Abbie turned to me. "Since we're so close, we need to see the Tesselated Pavement. It's unique."

"What is that? I've never heard of it."

"Because of the tide and tremendous water washing over it, there's an area that looks like the tiled floor of a mosque or famous building. At low tide you can see it all stretched out before you. Of course, when the tide is in, it's not there. I think we're on a low tide, so we should get a good view."

She was right. It was intriguing.

"Tasmania is full of natural wonders, isn't it?"

"Yes, and did you know that it was originally called Van Diemen's Land? He was the governor general of the Dutch East Indies."

"Why did they change it?"

"Since his name sounds like 'demon' and it was a penal colony for Britain convicts from 1825 to 1853, they wanted to remove the unsavoury criminal connotation. Free people were now settling in Van Diemen's Land and didn't want to be thought criminals, since the penal colony didn't close until 1877. Abel Tasman was the first European to find the island, so they renamed it after him instead."

"Interesting."

"There are many more natural wonders around here. Do you want to see them?"

"You bet."

As we travelled and toured over Tasmania, I certainly was amused by the town names.

"Egg and Bacon Bay, Paradise, Snug, Promised Land, Penguin, Elephant Pass, Doo Town—you have some funny names here."

Abbie shrugged. "You get used to them and don't think about it. But I admit, I'd not like to have to put 'Hell's Gates' as my mailing address."

I laughed. "Me neither! Telling people I live in Paradise would be much more enjoyable. Even saying I live in Nowhere Else would seem a bit depressing. Why would anyone name a place Hell's Gates?"

"Most places got their name for a reason. Hell's Gates is a harbour town, and it's so rocky and treacherous, many ships have wrecked there. But it's mainly named that because of the terrible conditions on the penal colony."

"You said we're headed to Devil's Kitchen next. Why that name?"

"Wait until we get there and you'll see. But just remember, everywhere we're going now is a 'walk at your own risk' place. Please do not get too close to the edges of these ravines and cliffs. It's at least two hundred feet down and many jagged rocks along the way."

She was right. As we hiked around the Tasman Arch, stopped at the blowhole to hear the whistle of the ocean blowing like a whale, and stood in silence on top of the Devil's Kitchen, I could visualize why the natural wonders we gazed upon had such names. The Remarkable Cave was a bit scary. We had 150 steps to get down into this vertical cave, again at our own risk. Since the tide was just starting to come in, we were able to go down safely.

Abbie stopped me on the last dozen steps. "We need to wait. The water will come rushing in, and I'm not sure how high it's going to soar. Once it does that and goes out, we'll go down onto the rock. We can see straight out into the ocean."

So we waited, and sure enough, soon we heard a sound like a train. *Whoooossshh!* The cave below us was filled with water. Within a few minutes, it drained out and we dropped down. As the tide receded, we could look down a long, narrow tunnel straight out into the ocean. Suddenly the view went totally gray. I shrieked and we jumped for the stairs. We stood there as the water whooshed in and out. After a few times, we realized even standing on the big rock at the bottom, we'd be okay. It'd only get our feet wet. But it took nerve for me to stand there hearing that sound and feeling the rush come at you.

"Had enough?" Abbie turned to me.

"You bet. I've never wanted to die by drowning." I was glad I'd experienced this but was more than happy to scramble up to higher ground.

We planned a full day out when we hiked Cradle Mountain. God was so good, as we managed to hit one of the few days when the sun shone the entire day.

Abbie looked at me when we got out of the car. "How do you feel?"

"Fine. Why?"

"There's easy and hard hiking on this mountain. It's only twelve kilometres for the full circular hike, but it's classified as difficult and can take from five to eight hours if you go the whole way. So what do you want?"

"Can we turn back?"

"Oh, yes, and a couple places there are shorter circuits, if we want to shorten it."

"Well, let's take our backpacks and food and see how far we go."

"Sounds good."

The beginning was easy and beautiful. We hiked by the Twisted Lakes and through the Ballroom Forest, and again, the name fit. It was gorgeous and cool and full of massive trees and elegant manferns. We had little flags we could follow to stay on our trail. But in the middle of the Ballroom Forest, I suddenly lost sight of any flag.

"Abbie, the trail ends."

"It can't. There's got to be a trail continuing on." We hunted around, and then Abbie chuckled. "You're only looking around. Look up."

I followed her gaze and, sure enough, about thirty feet straight above us we saw the little yellow flag. "Straight up? How do we do that?"

Abbie planted her foot on a root. "See all these roots sticking out of the tree. They make excellent foot and handholds." As I continued staring up, she added, "The trail did say arduous, remember? Do you want to quit?"

I shook my head from its stupor. "No, let's try."

It actually was a lot easier than I thought, but I was glad Abbie had gone first. As I reached the top and ducked under a limb to crawl out onto the ground, my backpack caught in the limb.

"Ugh!" I groaned as I slammed to a stop, half stuck between the ground and the tree limb.

Abbie turned around and laughed. "You look a bit like a turtle."

I grimaced. "Just remember that it's your sandwiches also that are being squished flat." She leaned over me and the tree and managed to slip the backpack off my shoulders so I could ease my way under and stand again.

After the cool of the ballroom, the heat and glare from the rocks made me quite hot as we went through that stretch. Thankfully there were lots of little lakes along the way, and I kept refilling my water bottle to keep hydrated. We stopped in the shade at one to eat our lunch. As we looked back, I could see a faint trail way back down in the distance.

"Is that where we used to be?"

"Yup, and that's where we have to return to by and by." Abbie grinned at my moan. "But we're over halfway around already, so we'd better keep going!"

We did, but as we came back down on the other side, it was a lot of scrub brush and through swamp, so we got quite scratched up. When we wearily staggered back into the car parking lot, I looked at my watch.

"My legs will never forgive me, but we did it in five hours exactly."

Abbie wearily lifted her water bottle in accolade. "Since it can take up to eight hours for this hike, we are intrepid hikers to make it in the minimum time allotted."

It was probably the quietest drive home we'd ever done. We were both scratched, sunburnt, insect bitten, and dead tired—but we'd seen some phenomenal scenery, and that made it a great day.

We also did some easier days, such as attending the Burnie Ag Show, which was similar to our agricultural shows in Manitoba, and we attended a New Tribes Mission dinner. Some evenings we just went to the beach with the youth group and sang while watching the Southern Cross, or during the full moon had barbecues and games. There was so much to do and see in such a small area of space compared to my province, where you have to drive for hours to get to something. I felt like Abbie truly showed me her homeland during my time there.

Chapter 31

Of course, life wasn't all just about sightseeing. School was intense, and a lot of time went into my work there, too. I found it rather stressful coming in to cover for another teacher for the last few months. She was going on maternity leave so hadn't had the energy to keep up with the fourteen second to fourth graders. I walked into quite a few disciplinary problems. I preferred working with students older than these, so sometimes I was at a loss to know the best way to handle so many younger children. One boy was a bawler when he didn't get his own way. After a five-minute session of crying, I went to him.

"Okay, that's it."

He looked up and smiled. "Okay? I don't have to do the math?"

"No. Okay, you can go sit outside and cry."

His eyes rounded. "What?"

"Stand up." He stood and I picked up his chair and walked to the door. I placed the chair outside and motioned to him to sit on it. "There you go. Cry all you want. When you're done, you're welcome to come back inside." He was so astonished, he did what I said.

Pretty soon the door opened. "Miss Kanner, it's cold out here. Can I come in?"

I didn't even look up from the student I was helping. "Depends."

"On what?"

"If you're done crying."

"I am."

"Great. Come on in and get to work on the math, please." He did and soon had the work done. I stopped by his desk. "Hey, great job, and very neatly done." He looked up at me and had an honest, nice grin for me.

I had a grandmotherly lady helping me, and she just looked at me. "I don't believe that."

"Believe what?"

"How you dealt with that. We've had so much trouble with that boy crying all the time. We never thought of doing something like that."

I shrugged. "You never know what will work. You try something and hope it helps. If not, then you try something different. Life as a teacher is like playing a gigantic game of chess. You look at the life of the students and make moves you hope will help them grow into mature, responsible adults. Sometimes you win, sometimes you lose."

The school was mostly a family-run operation, so sometimes that caused a bit of stress. When the administration and the principal are father and son, it's intimidating trying to lodge a complaint when you're frustrated about something. So I stepped on toes a few times over things I didn't understand. Being a foreigner has its pros and cons. You can be brushed off for having such odd ideas, but you also can be forgiven for not knowing how it's done.

Since I was there for the last term before school let out for summer in December, the ACE convention was the big event coming up. It was a four-day event that my young students attended during the day, but the older students stayed overnight. When they found out that I enjoyed music, I was given a couple of pieces to play for the students' solos and duets. I didn't mind, except that I was simply told I would do it with only a week's notice. I'm not the greatest pianist if it's a specific, complex piece. So that was a bit stressful.

I was excited about seeing how convention was done in Australia, since we'd always been involved in convention in my Alberta school. My bubble burst when Abbie burst into my classroom after school one day.

"Have you heard the news?"

"No, what?"

"You and I have been chosen to be the chaperones for convention."

I looked at her. "Why does that upset you? I expected we'd have to be in charge of the kids all day."

She shook her head. "No, not that. We're to be on campus the whole time to chaperone the high schoolers."

"What?" I jumped to my feet. "No. They can't do that to us. I've never had any involvement with the high school here. How many students is that?"

"About fifty. They stay overnight, and from what I heard last year, there was quite a bit of trouble. Some of them are a bit wild."

"But why us? That's not our responsibility."

Abbie grimaced. "You have a reputation for being a strict teacher, so they think you can keep them under control."

"The principal and his wife run the high school. Why can't they stay overnight?"

"They will, but they say they have too many other responsibilities to also watch over the students."

That was one of the times I stepped on a few toes, but I didn't get out of it. We were the chaperones. It made for an exhausting four days. During the day I was busy making sure my class got to the competitions they were involved in. I also had to keep them out of mischief. They'd been told the water areas were off limits, but Tim fell into the duck pond the one day and I had to fish him out. Since he was a day student, he had no extra clothes, so I took him to my bunk and he wrapped himself in my sleeping bag. He had to stay there until his clothes dried out on the line, so I figured that was poetic justice.

Once our students were gone for the day, Abbie and I turned our attention to the high schoolers. It's intimidating to suddenly be in charge of a lot of students when you haven't had any rapport built up. It wasn't that they were bad kids, but they weren't used to being told what to do, and we butted heads a few times.

Everyone was supposed to be in the evening rallies. I noticed a bunch of boys were missing, and then I had girls leaving. I stopped one.

"Where are you going?"

"To the loo (washroom)." I let her go, but after another half dozen all needed the loo and no one came back, I turned to Abbie.

"We've got a problem."

"What should we do?"

"Let's go."

We slipped outside and, sure enough, discovered all the girls in the boys' cabin. I was very nervous about what to do or say on the walk over there, but when I opened the door and saw them all, suddenly I was furious. Why was it that I, the foreigner, had to do all the nasty disciplinary stuff? I stood in the doorway and spoke.

"Excuse me, but just what do you think you're doing out here?"

Someone spoke up. "Just talking."

I snorted, as it was obvious they were planning more than that. "Yeah, well the meeting isn't over, and you didn't have permission to leave, so get back over there." I saw one girl try to slip away through the back door and raised my voice. "Excuse me, Bethany, but the meeting hall is the other way! Abbie, could you start listing these names for me so I know whose parents to talk to later." As I started calling the girls by name, there was a mad rush out the door.

We followed them out and Abbie exclaimed, "Wow, you were good. I didn't know what to do." I blew out a long breath and then realized the boys weren't behind us.

I turned around and stopped. "Boys, I'm waiting."

One voice called out, "I just have to get my blazer on."

We waited some more, but no one came out. So I marched up to the door and put on my best "enough" voice. "Boys, I live in a country that is forty-below-zero for months. Do you really want to see what a Canadian can do?"

That seemed to do the trick. The boys came walking out, and Abbie and I sheep-dog herded them back to the hall.

I figured I'd have some very angry teenagers, and although a couple of comments about the bossy foreigner floated around, Abbie surprised me as we were washing up our breakfast dishes.

"A couple of girls told me that you are okay." Abbie laughed at my look. "Yes, a few are mad, but you know how teenagers are. A lot of them just follow peer pressure, so there's only a couple of bad apples here. They just affect the others who don't know how to say 'no' to them. I think a few were relieved you keep on them like you do."

"Well, four nights of no sleep is not doing much for my disposition. I'll be so glad when this is over." I collected my dishes and started to leave the kitchen. This was one area that was so different from other conventions I'd attended. Here you had to bring your own cup, plate, cutlery, and even dish towel. Each person was responsible to wash and dry his/her own dishes after each meal. If you lost your stuff, that was your problem. Thankfully, Abbie had made me aware of it, so each of us had brought an extra set of stuff, just in case. I did loan it out to a student or two over the course of the week.

The older girls rallied around me after they found out I could braid hair. I spent a couple of hours helping them get hair done for the awards night program the last day, and all my disciplining seemed to have been forgotten. So it ended on a good note, but I was so thankful that we had a few days off with a long weekend at the end of the convention. It took that long to rejuvenate from the constant daytime activities and sleepless nights in a dorm with a bunch of girls.

Having done the time at convention, I was surprised when the principal approached me about chaperoning again.

"Stacy, I have a dozen students that made Honour Roll."

I was surprised. "That's nice, Darren."

"We wondered if you'd like to chaperone for the nine girls."

"What about your wife?"

"She can't make it this time. The girls asked if you could come instead."

I was surprised. "Me? They actually asked for me?"

He laughed. "Yes. You know them all from convention now, so would you do this? My wife and I thought you'd like to go, as you'll see a bit more of the country."

I nodded. "Sure, when would it be?"

"We'll leave Friday morning and return Sunday evening. We'll be in the Hobart area, and there's a church down there that will let us bunk out in their sanctuary for the two nights."

I agreed and ended up having a good time. We hiked Mt. Wellington and got an excellent view of Hobart, toured the Parliament building, and spent a long time in a Science Educational Centre. Of course, one evening we spent several hours in the Eastland shopping mall, as the girls all wanted to shop. The other evening the church hosted a barbecue for us. Our only problem on that trip arose when we went to leave. They had given us a key to come and go. After all the luggage was loaded and kids were piling in the van, I turned to Darren.

"Did you leave the key on the table?"

He groaned. "Ah, no. It's in my pants' pocket."

I frowned. "So why the groan? Dig it out."

He nodded at the van. Now I groaned. "Oh no. It's not the pants you're wearing, is it?"

He shrugged. "Nope, and my bag was the first loaded, so it's at the bottom."

After we hauled everything out, dug through, and found the key, he had me run it back in and lay it on the table while they reloaded. We all jumped back in, slammed the door, and pulled around the corner. Darren groaned again.

"What now?"

"I forgot. The gate is locked, and the key to open it is on the ring you just left in the church." I stared at him. He shrugged. "I know, I know. That's why I have my wife. She always remembers this kind of stuff for me."

An hour later, after some nasty scratches on my arm, we'd managed to pick open a lock and get my arm in far enough to unlatch the window. We had the skinniest kid slide through and get the key and walk out the front door. I refused to let that key out of my hand until the van was sitting outside the gated church, running and ready to leave. Then I went in one more time to lay the key on the table, lock the church, and then lock the gate and get into the van.

Just as we started to roll, one of the boys called out, "Hey, I gotta use the loo!" I whipped around and glared at him, and he grinned. "Just kiddin', mate!" They all laughed and we finally headed for home.

Although we did a lot of privilege trips just around the compound, playing soccer and so on, there were a few field trips off the property as well. We went to a waterslide park, attended a town and country fair, and visited a few businesses. One of the all-school events was going to Devonport to watch as *The Spirit of Tasmania*, a brand-new boat, sailed into the harbour to become the biggest, newest ferry to transport people between the mainland and this Apple Isle. It was a huge event, and I was so pleased I got to be one of the ten thousand people watching as she made her first sail into the harbour.

As the school year wound to an end, they had their annual beach picnic. That was an all-day affair out at the ocean. By then it was hot and sunny, so playing in the water made for a great day. I had all my students take their shoes and socks off. I wanted to make sure they didn't lose them, so I looked around carefully. There was a huge rock a ways out in the ocean that was as high as my head. I decided to put all the shoes up there, as there was no danger of losing that big rock.

The day leisurely passed along. Families had brought their own picnic lunch, with a barbecue planned for the evening. I wasn't responsible for my students, as everyone had family there, so I joined the massive cricket match.

Cricket was a game I found hard to play. It was too different yet too similar to baseball for me to keep it straight. Slade put me on his team so he could coach me on what to do. We played on the beach right in the ocean. It was so neat. As the tide slowly started to creep in, we'd be playing with water swirling around our ankles. When it got too hard to run, we'd pull up the stakes, move in a hundred feet, and keep on playing.

As tea time drew nigh, we finished the game and flopped down. Soon one of the students came to me. "Miss Kanner, where did you put my shoes?"

I sat up. "Over on the rock right there." I pointed, and to my horror saw way out in the water a small, triangular point sticking out of the water and a bunch of black specks bobbing out to sea. "Aaah! What happened? That was a huge rock!" My commotion caught everyone's attention and Slade came over.

"What's wrong?"

"I put everyone's shoes on a massive rock so they'd be safe! It was higher than my head."

I blushed as everyone started to laugh. Slade made an attempt to hide his grin. "I'm sorry. We forget what a landlubber you are. You never leave things on rocks at the ocean when the tide is out. What goes out will come in."

"Fine time to tell me," I grumbled. "I just sent fourteen pairs of socks and shoes to a watery grave."

Some of the parents were not amused, but thankfully most of them weren't too upset. "What can you expect from a foreigner?" seemed to be the general consensus.

As the days got hotter and my time got shorter, I began to panic on what to do, how to get home, where to go. Every avenue I explored seemed to fizzle out on me. I felt so helpless. But then in the middle of November the Canmores had me over. Jasmine started the conversation.

"Have you made a decision yet on how and when to go home?"

I sighed. "I'm so frustrated. I've tried different things, and nothing seems to work out. So I decided to just buy a plane ticket straight home, but I couldn't access the money I needed that day. I don't know what God's trying to tell me!"

They exchanged glances, and then Slade spoke up. "Well, the thing is, we've decided to move back to the mainland. We've discussed it, and if you want to spend a few weeks on the mainland, we'd have room for you in our vehicle. We'll be leaving December 23 and taking the boat across to Melbourne."

Jasmine piped in. "We'll go to Canberra first. That's about a twelve-hour drive. But then our family goes to the beach for a couple of weeks. If you'd like to spend a week at the ocean, we'd have room there as well."

"Oh my! That would be so fun! I've also received word from Darla, the lady that met me at the airport. She invited me to spend a week with her if I got to Sydney, so maybe this could all work together!"

With that, we started making plans. Slade took me with him the next day to book our tickets on *The Spirit of Tasmania*. He grinned at me. "You got to see this brand-new boat arrive, and now you'll have the privilege of riding her in the first month of her arrival.

When we booked the tickets, I was a bit nervous. Slade and his family needed a cabin to themselves, so I was slotted in a four-female-share cabin. I wasn't sure who I'd end up having to share a bunk with but decided to worry about that later.

As always, the last couple of weeks before departure just flew. December 15 was the awards night. As a thank you, the ladies all received bouquets. I was stunned at the huge, plum-coloured exotic armful I received. It was absolutely beautiful and the biggest bouquet I'd ever seen in my life. December 16 was a school picnic, the seventeenth the staff dinner, and then on the eighteenth I had my hardest task. I had to say goodbye to Alison. She was headed home and wasn't planning to return to teach the next year either. It was gut-wrenching, as these goodbyes are fairly dead-end. Seeing each other again was highly improbable. But at least the memories couldn't be taken from me.

On December 19 the Hayes invited both the Canmores and myself to dinner after church to say goodbye. On the twentieth I did the last shopping and finished my packing so that I could spend the entire day on the twenty-first helping Jasmine finish packing and loading for her family. On the twenty-second my helper, Giselle, had her birthday and invited me for the day for fun, food, games, and last goodbyes.

Chapter 32

After eight intense days of go, go, go and the stress of saying goodbye, it was almost a relief to climb into the van with the Canmores and head down the driveway. I looked back as we drove beneath the overhanging gum trees. "Goodbye, Tasmania. It was an amazing few months." I kept my eyes facing out the window so the family couldn't see my tears. Then I drew a deep breath and faced forward to the next adventure.

However, the goodbyes weren't over. Although we had to be at the boat by 4:00 p.m., we didn't board until 5:30, as there were over a thousand passengers and about three hundred vehicles to load before departure. So a lot of Geneva people had driven over to see the Canmores off and spent the hour with us as we waited. More goodbyes again—I am so bad at them. Finally we were called on deck and soon had parked. We headed to the passenger deck to watch Tasmania slowly disappear from sight before trying to find our cabins. Because I was in a single female cabin, while the Canmores had a family unit, we weren't close to each other. With the boat being eleven stories high, I was frightened I'd never find them again, so Slade came with me and then walked me back to their cabin and made a map for me.

When I went back to my bunk for the evening, I was pleasantly surprised to find only one other passenger in our cabin. It made it so nice. Had there been four of us, we would have been extremely cramped. This way we each took a lower bunk and heaved our overnight cases on the top bunk. It took a bit to get used to the sway of the boat as I climbed into bed for the night.

The next morning we met bright and early, as we had to be one of the first ones off the boat. What a difference—both in temperature and in people. Tasmania was casual and laidback, while Melbourne was a frantically-paced city. Between exchanging sea legs for land legs again, the temperature change, and the huge number of people around, I felt like I'd just been zoomed through a time-warp tunnel.

The Canmores' van did not have air conditioning, and throughout the twelve-hour drive we stopped just for toilet breaks. The temperature reached thirty-four degrees Celsius, and I started to develop a heat headache. I still felt a bit dizzy from the boat's motion as well.

Slade grinned at me as we stopped for lunch. "You ever hear of Gundagai?"

"No." I shrugged. "Why?"

His boys laughed as he explained. "This is famous for the dog that sat on the tuckerbox (lunch bag). There's a statue here and a poem and a song that's nearly as well-known as 'Waltzing Matilda' is." He made sure I stopped and read the inscription on the statue.

I was able to shop a bit and found a poster with the poem "The Man from Snowy River" on it. I showed it to the Canmores.

"Now this impresses me more than your tuckerbox dog. They've even made a movie from this poem about the Australian Outback."

Slade was a guy that really knew his facts. "Have you looked closely at our five-dollar bills?"

"Not really. Why?"

"If you look very closely on the bottom of the bill, there's a line from that poem. The poem is so famous that even the movie has a lot of the direct lines from the poem in it. You don't often see movie companies sticking so close to the original."

Jasmine joined in. "If that story intrigues you, we'll be passing by the Snowy Mountain Range on this trip, so you can see the area you're talking about."

One of the boys piped up. "Are we going to stop at the big hydro plant?"

"Not this time, son. We have a long run to get to Canberra, and Stacy here is already wilting in our heat."

He was right. After twelve hours on a boat, followed by twelve hours in a non-air-conditioned vehicle in thirty-five degrees Celsius weather, I was not only wilting but past roasted. When we got out of the car at our final destination, I was weaving and felt sick to my stomach. Jasmine was worried.

"Stacy, I think you might have a touch of sunstroke."

"Whatever it is, it's nasty. I feel like I'm in a bubble that has no up or down to it. It's a horrible sensation."

"You go lie down for a while and see if that helps."

Christmas morning I went to the church service with them. Partway through I got hot and sweaty and so lightheaded I nearly keeled over. They got me back home and I went back to bed. When I got up to go to the bathroom, I just fell to the floor. The only way I could go down the hall was by putting my back to the wall and sliding along on my rear end because I couldn't tell where the floor or the ceiling was, and the boundaries of left and right didn't exist. At the time I'd never heard of vertigo, but in retrospect, I probably had it. It was one of the most miserable Christmases I'd ever had, and I felt too horrible to even care. Mind you, the Canmores had their frustrations that day, too. Their oldest son, Jerry, fell and broke his arm, while the younger one, Jesse, received a huge gash across his forehead, so they spent the evening at the hospital.

On December 26 I stayed in bed all morning. By mid-afternoon I was able to walk a bit, although I still weaved.

Slade couldn't resist teasing me. "I want to take you out and show you a few of the sites of Canberra, but if you see a coppa (police officer), please sit and don't move until he's gone."

"Why?"

He laughed. "You're walking like a drunken sailor. He'll make us all take breath analysers if he sees you."

"Ha-ha. Not funny!"

While Jasmine stayed to pack up what they needed for the beach for two weeks, Slade and the boys took me on a sightseeing mission.

"You can't come to Canberra and not see what our capital of Australia looks like." Slade helped me into the vehicle. "We can do most of it by driving, so you don't have to walk too much. Many cities just kind of sprang up as settlers arrived, but this city was planned and designed before people moved in."

"Okay, let's try." When we got to the top of Mt. Ainslee and looked down on Canberra, I could see what he meant. The city was laid out in a symmetrical fashion that was neat to see. I also enjoyed seeing Parliament House and the War Memorial, among other things.

When we returned to his brother's house, Jasmine had everything ready for

Slade to load. I decided to use the bathroom before we headed to the camp they'd rented at the coast. The toilets over there weren't big, wide rooms like many Canadian ones are. They often had only the toilet in a small closet-like room. The washbasin was outside so that people could use it even if the toilet was occupied.

I entered the small facility and locked the door. To my dismay, it wouldn't unlock. I tried several times with no luck.

"Help, help!" I started pounding on the door. Soon Jerry came down the hall.

"Hey, Stacy, what's taking you so long? Dad says to hurry up, as we're ready to leave."

"I can't get the door open!"

Jerry snickered. "Unlock the latch."

"Very funny. Go get your dad. The lock is stuck." He ambled off. Soon Slade and his brother were outside the door.

"What's up, Stacy?"

"This stupid door won't open."

Slade's brother spoke up. "I'm so sorry about this. We've been having trouble with the lock, and I've been meaning to get another one. We just don't lock the door."

"Fine time to tell me that! Now what?" I could hear the men outside rattling the knob, discussing what best to do. Meanwhile, my claustrophobia had kicked in big time. I started sweating and gasping for air.

Slade heard me. "Stacy, what's wrong?"

"I'm locked in a closet and can't breathe, that's what's wrong."

"You have claustrophobia?"

"Duh! Give the man a cookie. For Pete's sake, stop discussing the matter and *do* something! Break down the door. Get a chainsaw. I don't care; just get me *out* of here!"

Slade chuckled. "Don't panic, Stacy. This is fixable. We just have to go get some tools and take the hinges off the door. Close your eyes and imagine your wide-open fields of Canada." He turned to his boys. "You boys stay here and tell her your jokes while your uncle and I go get the tools."

Jerry's voice came through the door. "Knock-knock ..."

I groaned but answered. "Who's there?"

"Boo."

"Boo who?"

"Boo-hoo, she's stuck in the toilet and can't get out." His little brothers laughed hysterically while I sighed and tried to breathe slowly.

Half an hour after I originally entered the small room, the door slowly started to move away. I jumped to my feet. The door stopped moving.

"Hey—what's wrong? Keep taking that thing off."

Slade's voice came through. "Uhm, everybody's here in the hall watching. Are you decent if we completely remove the door?"

"Slade! I've been in here half an hour—I ought to be done my business by now."

Everyone laughed, and to my blessed relief the door came off and I was free. I lunged out of there, twirled around, and spread my arms out. "Space. Freedom. The most beautiful words in the dictionary."

Jerry stared at me. "Hey, you're walking straight again!"

They all stared at me. I walked down the hall and turned. "Wow. That's the floor, this is the left wall, and there's the ceiling. I'm out of my bubble!"

Jasmine started laughing. "Only you, Stacy!"

"Only me what?"

"Only you could cure a case of vertigo by having a claustrophobic panic attack."

I have no idea if that's what did it, but I was fine again except for a sharp pain in my head. I was thankful to be out of that horrific bubble, although my fear of small spaces had ramped up again.

After the delay, we ended up having supper with them before climbing into the vehicle to head to the ocean. Since the Canmores' family tradition was to rent a campground complex for two weeks each year, I'd see this family again as well as meet many more. All of Slade's siblings and cousins and parents came to this ocean oasis. Some came only for a few days as they were able, while others stayed the full two weeks. I had made arrangements with Darla, one of the original ladies that met me at the Sydney airport, to go spend a week with her. So I'd be with Slade and Jasmine the first week and then get to spend a week in Sydney at her place as well.

Little Jesse grinned at me as we pulled out of his uncle's place. "You'll be happier now."

I looked at him. "Why do you say that?"

"We're right at the ocean. It's not as hot there, so your face won't be so red all the time."

Jasmine groaned. "Jesse!"

I shrugged. "It's okay. It's true, after all, so I hope the rest of what he said is true, too."

Jasmine nodded. "Yes. Unfortunately, this summer we're having a bad heat wave. It's not always forty-two degrees Celsius in the summer."

Slade added his two cents' worth. "When mainland knew you were coming, they decided to give you a warm welcome."

Jasmine elbowed Slade. "Ulladulla will be much easier on you. It's two and a half hours from Canberra. When we get to the coast, you'll still have to be careful about sunburn, but the ocean breeze makes life much more comfortable."

I smiled as we headed out of Canberra. That sounded wonderful to me.

Chapter 33

The Canmores were right. The coast was so much easier on my body heat wise. The complex they rented was right at the ocean. I quickly learned to decide to either go onto the beach early in the morning or late in the afternoon. From eleven o'clock to about four o'clock in the afternoon I didn't want to walk over the sand dune that separated our cabins from the water. The sand was so hot, even with sandals on it burned any part of my skin it rubbed against. The Canmore family was tougher than I. They could run over the sand and not seem to be bothered with burnt feet.

I couldn't get over the variety of parrots around the place. Jasmine noticed me watching them.

"Do you like birds?"

"No, not exactly, but I can't get over the vibrant colours your birds have. Look at that one—an emerald green body, sunshine yellow throat, and peacock blue head."

Jasmine nodded. "That's a Lorikeet. They are beautiful; some of them also have bright orange on them as well. It's a small parrot and probably one of our most colourful birds. I hope you don't mind birds."

I looked at her. "I don't have a specific love or hatred of birds. Why?"

She grinned. "You're going to hear a lot of bird calls and noises around here. It's part of the ocean's ambience. As well, today Slade's cousin arrives. Max and Connie are bringing Larry."

"Who's Larry?"

"They rescued a cockatoo that was hit by a car. He has only one leg and is a bit hostile to humans because of it, except for Max and Connie. He stays close to them, so he shouldn't bother you."

Jasmine was dead wrong. I don't know if it was because of my accent, but Larry developed a dislike of me, which soon became mutual. Every morning at 6:00 I'd suddenly feel this claw scrabbling and hopping on my head. "Hello, hello, I'm Larry." I'd make a swipe with my arm and he'd dance out of reach. "Ha. You missed. You're stupid." Parrots aren't supposed to understand the words they utter, but Larry had developed a sixth sense for saying the right words at the right time. As soon as I settled, he'd be back on my head. "Hello, say hello to Larry." Another swipe and miss and he'd chuckle. "I'm good, you're bad. Haaaah!" I'd throw my pillow at him and knock him over. "No fair! No fair!"

The family thought it all quite humorous and didn't understand why he took such delight in tormenting me. I couldn't believe anyone would pay good money for such an annoying bird.

The week was a come and go and do as you please, which was relaxing. The meals were planned for a specific time, and different ones took turns making them. If you were there, you ate together. If you weren't, you fended for yourself.

The second morning there, Jasmine turned to me. "Ready to boogie board?"

My jaw dropped. "What on earth is that?"

Her sons overheard us. Jerry piped up. "It's the greatest fun ever. You ride the waves."

Since I'm not a swimmer, I immediately started to demur. "I appreciate that, but I don't have any boogie board, whatever that is."

Jasmine laughed. It's the same thing as body boarding. You take the board out into the waves, catch a wave, and ride it back onto shore. It's great fun. Just make sure you ride a blue or white wave. Don't catch a brown one."

"What's wrong with a brown one?"

"If it's brown, that means it has sand in it, which in turn means there's enough undertow in it to pull you under."

"Oh great, just what I wanted to hear."

She nudged me. "Come on. You can use Slade's board and I'll be with you. You can't leave here without at least trying it."

I followed her to the beach. As I looked at the waves higher than my head rolling in, I shrugged. "How do you even 'catch' a wave?"

Jasmine started to wade in. "Just keep on walking out. When a wave comes at you, duck under it. Once it's past, you'll find you're not out very deep. Keep ducking under the waves until you're at least waist deep. As the wave comes roaring toward you, jump up with your board, and the force will throw you on top of the crest so you can ride it in to shore."

I sucked in a deep breath and tried to stay just behind her and mimic her actions. Suddenly she called out, "Jump!" I shut my eyes and flung myself up. There was a whooshing sensation and the wind started whipping past my cheeks. I opened my eyes and laughed.

"Wow! What a feeling." The first few seconds were fantastic, but then I began to pick up speed. *Rats! I forgot to ask her how to slow down.* I pushed against my board, hoping it would act like a brake. Instead, I suddenly started going faster and faster. I pushed harder. *S-t-t-o-p-p!* My two long braids slapped in front of me, and I couldn't talk. Soon the beach came roaring toward me. *At least I'll stop when I hit sand*, my brain tried to encourage me. However, I was going so fast when the wave threw me onto the sand, I just flew across it. I dropped my feet to brake. *Aaaaah! Massive rug burn!* I pulled my feet back up as sand whipped into my mouth and my eyes. *Duh, Stacy. Now's the time to push down on the board.* I did that, and I immediately stopped. Unfortunately, my two braids happened to be underneath the board, and I nearly scalped myself as I did a somersault off the board and onto the sand. "Ouch!" I blearily gazed around as I tried to rub the grit out of my eyes. The Canmore boys were staring at me.

Jerry spoke animatedly. "Wow. Doing tricks your first time out. Cool!"

I kept brushing sand off and didn't bother answering.

Jasmine came over. "For a beginner, you certainly didn't hesitate to pick up speed."

I glared at her. "Pick up speed? I was trying to slow down. That was scary!"

She grinned sheepishly. "Oops, I guess I forgot to tell you. You can't really slow down a lot, but you can always pick up more speed by pushing down on the board." She helped me brush off. "Ready to try it again?"

I gave it a few more tries. It was fun, but it was also exhausting, and I'm not a huge water fan, so I was more than happy to hand the board off to someone else and go back to just playing in the water and sitting under the umbrella and reading.

New Year's Eve we went into Ulladulla to shop and go to the rock pool. It's a swimming pool set into the ocean. At high tide it fills up and was excellent for just swimming, as the surf's too violent for much swimming in the ocean. We ended the year with a highly competitive volleyball game between the families, with Larry as the highly vocal 'ref.'

On Sunday after church there was a baptism at the ocean. I found it fascinating to see one performed in the midst of crashing, rolling breakers. They were doing fine until the preacher went to put the man under. As he bent over, an unexpected wave came rolling in and caught him just right. *Both* men went under and came up sputtering.

I turned to Jasmine. "So who baptized whom?" She shook her head at me, but my crazy sense of humour couldn't let go of that image. The rest of the day I randomly started giggling.

Little Jesse got worried. "Are you having sunstroke?"

"No. Why?"

"'Cause you just start laughing out loud and there's nothing funny happening." That made me laugh even more.

On January 3, I packed what I needed for a week's stay with Darla and left the rest of my luggage with the Canmores. I caught a ride with Max and Connie, who had to leave. Their cousin, Anise, was also headed home. Since we'd gotten along well this week, I was grateful she'd be with me part of the way.

They dropped us off in Thirroul with just enough time to buy tickets and jump on the train. When we got to the Central Station in Sydney, I was quite intimidated. There were at least twenty platforms, with trains leaving every couple minutes.

Anise yelled in my ear. "Follow me." We walked over to a big board and she looked at it for a few minutes. "Hey—there's a train leaving for Campbelltown in two minutes. Run!"

We dashed off like a pair of jackrabbits and lunged up a flight of stairs. "There!" She pointed at a train. "It's just ready to pull out. Get on, or you'll have to wait a while."

I jumped on the step and looked back. "How do I know when to get off?"

"It's the last stop on the run. There'll be a big sign that says Campbelltown." The train gave a jerk, and I hopped into the compartment. "Have f-u-n-n ..." were the last words from Anise's mouth as I waved madly then plopped into a seat.

Fly to Australia without a clue where to go. Spend the last week in Australia without a clue where you're going. Way to go, Stacy.

Since Campbelltown was considered a part of Greater Western Sydney, it took nearly an hour to get there on the train. But the train system was extremely efficient. It made frequent stops along the route, but you had about half a minute to hop on or off, and it was gone again. Knowing mine was the last stop, I was able to relax after someone told me it'd take me about an hour.

When I debarked at the last stop, I saw there were three different platforms with lots of people and no sign of Darla. I sighed. *Déjà vu. At least this time I have money and a phone number.* I marched along blindly until I found a phone booth and dialed.

Soon Darla answered. "Hello?"

"Hey there. It's me."

"Oh my. Nice to hear from you. Where are you?"

"Don't know. On some platform at a train station in Campbelltown."

Silence reigned for a moment before Darla laughed. "My dear, don't tell me we did this to you again. I'm so sorry. I knew you were coming today; I just didn't know what train you were catching."

"Anise was supposed to call you to tell you, as I didn't have time if I wanted to catch this train. I guess she forgot."

"Well, you won't have to wait very long this time. I'll call Julia and we'll be right there."

It was good to see both of the women again and fill them in on the things that had happened to me since I last met them.

Darla didn't own a vehicle, but between the bus and the train, she easily took me all around during my week with her. Just down the street from her place was the bus stop that took us to the train station in ten minutes. We left early one morning and headed into downtown Sydney to do some serious sightseeing. I nearly melted in the heat but got to walk over the Sydney Harbour Bridge, explore the Opera House, and go down into "The Rocks," a quaint historic area established in the 1800s. Souvenir shopping was a must, and I finally found the Squatter game I was looking for. We even toured the Botanical Gardens. I believe that is the only garden I've been to where I entered the orchid conservatory to cool down. Most places your glasses steam up when you get into the specialized plant places.

When we finally staggered back onto the train and could sit for an hour in a cooled compartment, Darla explained.

"You hit a problematic time in our history to be here. First off, we're in the midst of a heat wave like we haven't experienced in a very long time. But last week Sydney started burning. They think an arsonist torched the posh area. With this heat wave and the winds, it's gotten out of control."

I nodded thoughtfully. "That makes sense, then. All day I felt like I smelt burning garbage."

She added. "Plus, there have been bushfires that are getting out of control. It's quite worrisome."

Despite that worry, she gave me a week to remember. Her daughter picked us up in her car one day and took us to the Wildlife Park. They gave me a special type of handkerchief to wear around my neck. You soak it in water and it helps to keep you cooler and hydrated a bit better. It was forty-one Celsius, so I admired their fortitude in making sure I got to sightsee when it was so blistering hot. The car wasn't air-conditioned, and neither was Darla's house. Since they were going out of their way to be such gracious hosts, I tried not to complain about the heat. When we went to get back into the car, the thermometer said forty-five degrees Celsius, and I nearly blistered my backside on the seat.

I spent as much time in front of her fan as I could in the evenings. As each day went by, it got harder to breathe as the smoke from the fires around us filtered over. I found it interesting to watch.

"What are you looking at?" Darla questioned me one morning when she caught me staring out the window.

"I find it fascinating how your smoke looks so different from our forest fires. Yours are such a whitish-grey colour. I wonder if it's because gum and eucalyptus trees are burning instead of pine and spruce."

She laughed. "You come up with the most interesting thoughts and concepts."

After the fourth day of forty-plus weather, we headed for the mall and spent the day shopping inside an air-conditioned building. That was wonderful—until we had to come out and get hit with the heat.

During this time I'd been trying to call my parents to let them know my arrival date and time to pick me up in Winnipeg. As I couldn't get through and couldn't get through, I became a bit worried. That seemed so strange. Finally, knowing Dad needed to have my arrival schedule, I decided to call in the middle of the night, his time. I hated to wake him up, but no matter when I called during the day his time, no one answered. Finally, this time he did.

"Hello, who is this?" He sounded awful.

"Dad, it's me. Are you okay? I've tried all week to call and couldn't get through. That's why I'm calling you at this time."

"Do you have your ticket home?"

"Yes."

"Good."

"Dad, you sound awful. I know it's the middle of the night, but is something wrong?" There was a pause in the line. "Dad? What's going on?"

His voice sounded so weary and shaky. "We didn't know how to get a hold of you. Your mom has congestive heart failure. She's been in the hospital this past week, and we aren't sure yet if she's going to make it."

I was stunned. I knew Mom had a weak heart, but this blindsided me. "What should I do?"

"If you're coming home in a couple of days, there's nothing to do. Just pray and leave it in God's hands. Try not to worry, Stacy. In some ways I'm glad I couldn't let you know so you could enjoy your last weeks over there. If she pulls through, then you'll be home to help take care of her in a few days, and that will be a great help."

I gave him my details for meeting me and hung up.

The next morning Jasmine called me. "Hey, just wanted to check in with you before we come to get you. Have you been watching the news about the fires?"

"Yes! It's getting hard to breathe with all the smoke around here."

She laughed. "Well, it was more than hard to breathe down here. The fire hit the camp. We turned on all the garden hoses, and the men took turns hosing the vans to keep the gas tanks from exploding."

I gasped. "Are you all okay?"

"Yes. We grabbed food and water and headed into the ocean. We stayed in the water for five hours and prayed. It was a strange place for a full-length prayer meeting, but I was thankful we had it!"

To my shame, my thoughts immediately flew to my souvenirs. "Did my suitcases make it?"

She laughed. "Yes, and so did the van they were in. With the men keeping the vans wet, they are intact. Even the cabins all were saved. The wind shifted, the fire jumped, and somehow the entire campground survived, but the next place down the road didn't."

"I'm so glad you all are okay. That was a real answer to prayer."

"We're getting packed to head to Sydney. I'm going with the boys, and Slade will swing by and pick you up after he drops his brother off. We'll stay with Slade's mum in South Sydney. She's in a safe area so far."

It was hard to say goodbye to Darla. We'd had a great time together and saw many things, despite the heat and the fires. On our way back into Sydney, we couldn't take the proper road, as the fire was too close. So I got to see a bit more of the area than expected, as we had to go on a long detour to make it to the area we needed to get to. It wasn't fun to spend the extra time on the road, as it was so hard to breathe, but we made it safely.

The next morning we gals took the train up to Circle Quay and went through a burnt out area. It was a sobering reminder of how quickly life can change as we stared at the bleak area that had been a thriving community just a few days earlier. From the train we switched to the ferry and sailed out to Manly.

"Are you a good seawoman?" Janie, Slade's mum, asked me shortly after embarking.

"I don't know. We don't have many seas on the prairies where I come from."

"Well, going through 'The Heads' is the best part, but it's pretty rough."

I nodded and took a firm grip on the edge of the boat. She was right. It was a bit like riding a roller coaster as we rolled and tossed with the waves. As we dropped down into a few of the troughs, it felt like I was going to be tossed overboard if we dipped any farther.

Manly is a huge tourist town and full of tiny shops. As we browsed our way down the streets, we eventually ended up on the beach. It was a fun experience, but I was tired after a full day outside.

On my last day in Australia, Slade and his boys took me to Botany Bay.

I was enthusiastic. "Hey, this is the spot where James Cook first landed and 'discovered' Australia."

Slade grinned. "You know your history. Do you remember the year?"

I shrugged. "Just before the 1800s, I think."

Slade liked history, too. "It was 1770. It was first called Stingray Harbour, but they changed it to Botany Bay because of all the amazing plants they found here."

"I didn't know that. I just know finding this place was what made Britain consider starting a penal colony on this land."

I was happy to get to see this last spot and enjoy my last night with this splendid family.

Chapter 34

As usual, the final goodbye at the airport on January 12 was heart wrenching. The Canmores had invested so much of themselves into my life for the past six months, and to know I'd probably never see them again just hurt.

However, once in the airport and through customs, my thoughts anxiously turned toward home. It had been five days since I'd managed to call home, so I had no idea if Mom was alive or dead. It made for an anxious ten-hour flight to Honolulu, the layover there, and then another five hours into Vancouver's International Airport. Between the worry of what might lie ahead and the sleeplessness of the long flights, I was a basket case. I made it through customs fine, then had to take my luggage, show my boarding passes to another guy, and drop my luggage back on another carousel. I had a plastic zip envelope in which I kept my money, my passport, and the boarding passes.

With my entire luggage on a cart, I pushed through the gateway, pulled my boarding passes from the envelope, and laid it on the top tray. I showed the man my passes and was cleared to move on. I tugged my two big suitcases onto the rolling belt, grabbed my carry-on stuff, shoved the cart in with the others, and headed up an escalator. Since I came in on an international flight and had to transfer over to the domestic terminal, I had a ways to go.

Two flights up I went to put my boarding passes away. *A-aa-h, Stacy! You dunderhead.* As clear as day in my mind, I could see the envelope sitting on the top of the tray. *You left the most important stuff behind.*

I went racing back to where I'd come out. I was frantic. The doors were closed and locked with big "No Entry" signs on them. There was an older lady official close by, so I went to her.

"Ma'am, I left my passport and money on the cart."

She looked at my stressed-out face. "Oh dear, that's not good."

"Can I go back in there? I know exactly where I left it."

She sighed. "I can take you just into the baggage area, but the carts will be gone by now, and no one is allowed back into the customs area."

She took me back, and she was right. All the carts where I'd left mine were gone.

I tried not to cry. "Now what?"

She pointed me in the right direction. "Go down that corridor. You'll find a Lost and Found counter. Tell the man there exactly what is missing, just in case someone finds it and turns it in."

I did as she suggested, but the man was not helpful. "Sweetheart, this is an international airport. You'll never get that stuff back again—especially if you have money with it. Are you sure that you didn't put it in your bag somewhere? Maybe double check that."

I left him and found a women's restroom. I went into the wheelchair accessible one, as it was the largest, and ripped the carry-ons completely apart, but the envelope wasn't in it—which I already knew. I could see exactly in my mind where I'd left the envelope. After leaving the washroom, I wandered over to another airline counter. That lady suggested trying to look at the carts on this level.

"Do they interchange carts from the international entrance upstairs to these?"

She shrugged. "Not usually, but it's better to check these also."

I thanked her and found a stack of carts. Since they were shoved tightly together, I suddenly thought, *What if the envelope fell onto the floor?* So I dropped to my hands and knees and started checking the floor. As I shuffled along staring at the floor, in my vision I suddenly saw a pair of shiny black shoes. As my eyeballs slowly moved up the black pants, my heart thudded. Finally I gazed into the eyes of a security guard.

"May I ask what you are doing crawling around on the floor?"

"I'm sorry, sir. I'm just looking for my passport."

"Where did you lose it?"

"Two floors down and several corridors over."

His eyebrows shot up. "And you expect to find it here?" Put that way it did sound ridiculous. He continued. "Your best bet is to go back to where you lost it."

He was frowning, so I decided it wasn't worth explaining what I'd already done. I got up and headed in the direction he'd pointed. As I passed the desk I'd stopped at, the lady looked at me and I shook my head. I checked at the Lost and Found, but it hadn't come in. Finally I came up to my original lady. As she looked at my woe-begotten face, she sighed.

"Look, honey, there's only one last thing you can try. See that door over there? The very top head guy for security is in that office right now. He's the only one with the authority to let you back in. He won't do it, but you can ask. You're religious, so I know you believe in miracles."

I was in such despair I was willing to take any nibble, no matter how small. As I stood at the door, I gave myself a lecture. *Stacy, just walk in there and calmly state what happened.*

I opened the door and the man looked up. "What do you want?"

I burst into tears and stammered. "Sir, I'm so sorry, but I've been very stupid."

He got up, came around the desk, and was very patient as I explained (again) my situation.

"You do know that even if I let you in, you'll never find your envelope. We have thousands of carts." I gave him a tearful nod, and he reached for a piece of yellow paper and scribbled something on it. After handing it to me, he made me leave the rest of my carry-on stuff with him.

"We don't want you to lose that as well, do we?"

I thanked him and went skipping back to the lady official. Her eyeballs nearly popped.

"He actually gave you permission to go back in?"

"Yep!"

"Follow me." She pulled out a huge ring of keys and started unlocking doors. "By the way, I talked to the cart boys. None of them have seen your envelope."

"Well, thank you for that." At the last main door, she had to unlock four special locks, and then I was back in the "holy of holies."

She motioned me to enter. "Good luck."

I walked in and several officials jumped to their feet. I waved the yellow paper and their astonished looks made me realize I indeed had been given a huge concession. When I told them I just wanted to look at the carts, one guy waved his hand.

"Where do you want to start?"

I looked around, and from wall to wall was a sea of carts. "I'll start here." I moved to the closest wall. After a few minutes of intense stares, the officials returned to their jobs.

Two hours later as I started working on the third wall, I spied something. Frantically tugging on the carts before it, I almost started crying for sheer joy as I stretched out my hand and picked up—my envelope. Looking inside it, both the passport and all the money were still there, just like I left it. I let out a *Y-a-h-o-o-o* that scared the officials straight up off their chairs. As they stared from my beaming face to the envelope in my hand, jaws dropped.

"You've got to be kidding! You actually found it?" An older man came forward and looked at it. "In all my years working here, I've never heard of this." He pointed upwards. "You must have a real 'in' with Someone."

That was the consensus as I retraced my steps. The lady official gasped when I skipped up to her and waved the envelope.

"You found it? Unbelievable!" She shook her head. "Make sure you go back and thank the head guy."

"Oh, I will, and thank you so much for all your help." I skipped away and stuck my head inside the office door. "Excuse me, sir, God is so good!" As he looked up and his jaw dropped, I added, "… and so are you!" I collected my carry-on bags amidst his exclamations of shock.

My next stop was to let the Lost and Found guy know. As I approached that counter, I saw a pillow sitting there. I thought, *Man, someone lost their pillow. Too bad, but if they only knew how lucky they were that it's just a pillow.* I got closer. *Although it's a very pretty pillow … the log cabin design is just like the one my grandma made me … and it's got a little hole in the very same corner as mine does!* I looked down at my carryon. *Hey, my pillow is missing—that must be mine!*

I stopped in front of the man. "Guess what—they let me into the back and I found my envelope, so you can mark it off in your books. Oh, and by the way"—I picked up the pillow— "thanks for finding my pillow. I didn't realize I'd lost it in the furor of trying to find my passport."

He grinned and leaned over the counter. "That was discovered in the ladies' restroom upstairs."

"Ah, yes! That makes sense. I went in there and flipped everything out of my bags looking for this envelope, even though I knew it wouldn't be there.

Guess I forgot to grab it on the way out. I was a bit uptight."

He chuckled. "How much longer are you in this airport?"

I glanced at my watch. In all the turmoil I hadn't thought about the time. "Oh, eesh, I had a five-hour layover, and now I have just under an hour. I'd better get to my gate. It's way over in domestic."

"Well, sweetheart, is there anything else we can find for you before you leave?"

I looked up into his grinning face and blushed, which made him laugh even more. Until then I'd been so frantic, I hadn't thought what I must seem like. Suddenly I realized how embarrassing this all was. I thanked him and beat a hasty retreat.

As I went zipping past all the officials who'd been kind enough to talk or suggest things to me in my search, I gave them a thumbs up, and they all got shocked expressions on their faces. I was thankful that I could leave this terminal with my embarrassing incident to continue my flight elsewhere.

However, even way over in the domestic terminal as I stood in line waiting to go through the screening area, my hair prickled. I felt like I was being stared at. I looked around and noticed several officials staring at me. "Is something wrong?"

One guy spoke up. "Are you that gal that lost her passport and money and actually found it several hours later?" I turned beet red and they all laughed. "Yep, guess you are. Do you realize how totally lucky you are? That just doesn't happen."

"God was good and people were kind—but how did *you* know about it way over here?"

Another lady piped up. "Honey, everyone's talking about it!"

I grimaced. "This is *so* embarrassing!" I left the area as quickly as I could and made my way to my gate. I found a deserted area, plopped onto a bench, and pulled out my diary. I wanted to record my euphoric feelings while everything was fresh in my mind.

As I scribbled away, suddenly a body pressed against mine, and an arm came around my shoulders. I froze in shock. From above my head a voice spoke.

"From the look on your face, you must be writing a love letter. If someone is stupid enough to send you away, he doesn't deserve you. I'll be glad to take his place."

I looked up and saw a very big, very intimidating man. *Ah, Lord! What do I do now? I'm all alone, and this guy is scary.*

I primly stated, "I'm not writing a love letter. I'm trying to describe my feelings after having lost my passport and money for four hours and then finding them in this airport."

The man immediately removed his arm, scooted a few inches away, and looked me soberly in the eyes. "Oh, man. I know exactly how you feel. I'm a drummer in a rock band and once lost mine when leaving a concert in Germany. Only it wasn't lost. I forgot the bass guitar guy had it in his backpack, and he went through customs before I remembered. It's a nightmare, isn't it?"

I was astonished how having a common ground totally changed the way I felt about that man, and the way he responded to me. We chatted a bit before he stood up to go.

As he left, he hesitated and then turned back. "Hey, I'm sorry for—well, you know."

I shook my head. "You know, you don't have to be like that. You're a nice guy inside. Why not let people see that?"

He shrugged. "Everybody expects me to be the big bad guy. Guess I try to live up to it."

"Just be yourself—a nice, neat guy, okay?"

He grunted. "I'll think about it." He moved on, and I finished my writing and headed to the gate. *The last leg; I'm almost home. What will I find?*

Chapter 35

I stepped off the plane in Winnipeg and headed for the escalator. As I rode it down to the main level, I looked around in shock. *Everyone looks like a polar bear! What seems so different about these people? I've only been gone half a year.* But then I realized everyone was staring at me. I looked at myself and it hit me. *Man! I'm in a t-shirt and light skirt, bare legs and sandals. Everyone here is bundled up in massive coats and boots.*

I asked the person beside me. "Excuse me, do you know what the temp is outside?"

He gave me a queer look. "It's minus forty-two degrees, lady. You're going to freeze if you try to go outside like that!" He looked me up and down. "Where'd you come from anyway?"

"Australia. It's forty-two degrees above zero there."

Just then I saw Jocelyn waving at me. "Stacy, here!" As I looked at her and Dad, my heart throbbed. Mom was missing. She'd never missed being at my departure or return before.

After the first furor of greeting, I glanced at Dad. "Mom?"

His strained smile seemed genuine. "They moved her out of ICU two days after you called. She's going to make it. We'll go straight to the hospital from here. She's anxious to see you again."

"Which hospital?"

"She's in Steinbach now."

I'd been on the road travelling and waiting in airports for thirty hours, so this swing from Winnipeg to Steinbach before the drive home would add another few hours onto my day, but I was anxious to see Mom also, so I didn't care. I turned to Jocelyn.

"Did you remember to bring my coat and boots?"

"Yep. They're out in the car."

"In the car? What good will that do me here?"

"Well, I didn't know you were going to dress like it's the middle of summer."

"Well, it was the middle of summer where I was."

Dad started laughing. I turned to him. "What's so funny?"

"You girls may not look like sisters, but you definitely act like it. Can you wait at least an hour before you get into it with each other?"

Jocelyn and I looked at each other and laughed as well. "Okay, but I need that stuff in here."

Jocelyn nodded. "I'll go get them." She cocked her head. "You actually have a tan! I don't think I've ever seen you with a tan. You always burn and fade."

"Yeah, for once I'm not the Victorian delicate skin miss, and it stands out even more, since nobody else here has a tan."

Once I was bundled up, I walked out the door. A freezing blast of air hit me. I gasped, which was the wrong thing to do.

Dad looked at me. "What's wrong."

"I think a pair of knives just stabbed into my lungs." I wheezed as I tried to catch my breath. The pain was incredible. I had no idea it would hurt like it did. For the next six weeks as I stayed home and helped Mom, I struggled to adapt back to the cold winter. I always considered myself a winter girl, but I barely stuck my nose out of the house if I didn't have to. It was too painful to breathe.

I had a joyful reunion with Mom, but brief so we wouldn't tire her out. The hour-long drive home was when everything hit. I felt almost incoherent from lack of sleep, stress, pain—but I was home.

Within a week, Mom was able to come home. Jocelyn had a job with home care so was the best one to oversee Mom's personal care. While she did that, I took charge of the house side of things—groceries, cooking, et cetera, so Mom wouldn't worry about Dad.

In between all the reminiscing of my time in Australia with my family and my struggle to reacclimatise, I began to question God.

Lord, what now? I can't stay here the rest of my life, but I don't know what to do.

Have patience.

I feel like I shouldn't go so far away right now, but I don't fit in here anymore, so where, what, how?

Pray and wait.

Lord, I'm not so good at that.

I know, My child.

This winter is killing me, Lord. I hurt every day.

Wait.

Ahh!

Within a week of that dialogue with God, Dad approached me.

"Stacy, your mom is doing better now, and I've noticed you're struggling with the climate change."

"Yeah, not much I can do about that except remember to switch countries only in spring and fall. A temp change of eighty-two degrees is not smart."

"Now might be a good time to take a short trip. This cold snap can't last much longer, and if you go away for a couple of weeks, it might be easier for you when you get back."

"Wow, I never thought of that. Where would I go?"

"South. Your brother's place is not as cold as here, and he can also use a bit of help in his garage."

"Okay. I'll look into it if you're sure you and Mom are okay here."

"We'll be fine."

Not only was my brother happy to have me come help a couple of days, but my good friend Sybil from Riverton happened to mention she had two weeks' vacation due her.

"Sybil, I'm headed south. Would you like to come along?"

We talked it over and made plans, and by the end of February we'd packed my little car and headed off for heat and adventure. We had my *Mennonite-Your-Way* book, which is a Mennonite-based book listing people willing to let you stay overnight at their place as you travel through their area. We arranged a couple of stops for when we weren't in an area where I had friends and relatives along the way. The farther south we went, the easier I could breathe, and it was a great two-week trip to solidify our ongoing friendship.

A few of the highlights were touring the Mark Twain place in Hannibal, Missouri, stopping at Dolly Parton's place in Tennessee, seeing Helen Keller's birthplace in Alabama, and touring a plantation in Louisiana. The two weeks flew by, and soon it was time to head north again.

"I'm sure glad we took this trip," I spoke to Sybil as we loaded the car. "I didn't realize how getting out of the deep cold would help. Normally I'm the one who prefers cold weather to hot."

Sybil laughed as we slammed the door shut. "I was surprised when you first talked about going south to warm up. But it's been a nice break, and hopefully the cold snap will be over soon."

We started the car and I pulled onto the highway. We hadn't gone far when Sybil gave a shout. "Oh no! I left my purse on the roof of the car."

I glanced over my shoulder and saw her purse just at the edge of the window. "No, you didn't. It's sitting there right behind you."

She twisted around and then yelled. "Stop! It's on the outside of the car."

I quickly pulled over and we got out. Her cloth strap had been caught just at the edge of the door. The speed of the car caused it to soar backwards just enough so that it looked to be sitting inside the car. "Wow! Is that good or what?"

Sybil looked through the purse, and nothing had fallen out. She laughed. "Well, I paid a good price for this purse, and now I see it was worth it. Had it been a cheap one, it might have ripped, and I'd have lost everything."

Shortly before arriving back in Manitoba, Sybil gave me another thought to chew on.

"Since you invited me on this trip, how would you like to go on one with me?"

"What are you planning?"

"I've been saving my money to go back to visit my family in Belize." She grinned. "If I'm careful, I should have enough to go for their Christmas vacation. If you're teaching school, that's the same time you have off."

I sighed. "That's my problem. It's the beginning of March already, and I don't have a clue what I should do next. Mom's getting better, so I won't be needed around home, yet I'm not sure I should go far away right now. I feel like I'm hanging over a cliff. I ask God and He says, 'Wait.' You know how bad I am at that."

She chuckled. "Yep. But if you think He's telling you to wait, then there must be a reason for it. Don't run ahead of God." We drove a while in silence before she spoke again. "I'm pretty serious about wanting to go back to where I was born again. So just keep it in mind; if you're around, you're welcome to come along."

"I'd love to go to Belize. I've never been there. If we go at Christmas time, then the weather shouldn't be too hot for me."

"I thought we just made this trip south to warm you up! Make up your mind."

I rolled my eyes. "I still don't like hot weather, but after such intense Australian heat, this severe cold has caused breathing problems. I made an eighty-two degree jump in thirty-six hours. That's too hard on a body. By the time next winter rolls around, I'll be back to normal, I'm sure."

We crossed the border and made it home without incident. I continued to pray about what I should be doing as I worked about the house. The next week the phone rang.

Jocelyn answered and then handed the phone to me. "It's for you."

I spoke into the mouthpiece. "Hello?"

"Hello. This is the Red Lake school calling. We heard a rumour that you were back in this country looking for work. Is this true?"

"Yes, I've just returned from teaching in Australia and hope to find a school closer to home."

"We have an opening for a teacher next year in the same grade five to eight level that you had seven years ago. Would you be interested?"

We talked a bit longer and I hung up the phone. Mom looked at me. "What's wrong?"

I sank down beside her. "You know how sometimes you think God doesn't know what He's doing, and then bingo, exactly what you need suddenly happens?"

Mom chuckled. "God is the God of miracles today just like in Bible times. How has He answered prayer this time?"

"I've got a school for next year if I want it, and it's at Red Lake, so only eight hours away in case I want to come home on the weekends."

Mom patted my hand. "See, honey. When God says wait, something is coming. This sounds like a perfect spot for what we need right now."

I contacted Sybil the next day. "Hey, you'll never guess what!"

"What?"

"I'm going back to Red Lake in September to teach."

"Cool! That means you won't be too far away."

"Exactly. So I can start saving my pennies for Belize—if the offer still stands."

"Yes. I just talked to my cousins the other day and mentioned bringing a friend along, and they were fine with it."

I felt the most relaxed I'd been since stepping off the plane. Mom was alive. I had work for the upcoming year in an area I'd been to before, yet close enough to home to be able to spend long weekends with my family. To top it off, I even had another country and adventure to look forward to over the Christmas holidays.

I knelt by my bed that night. *Lord, thanks so much for your care, even when I get impatient.*

You're welcome, My child.

Help me to remember when the trials and troubles seem too much that's when I need to trust you the most.

I'll remind you.

Good night, Lord.

Sleep well, child.

I turned out my light and snuggled under the covers. I didn't know what the future would bring, but I was ready to enjoy being back in Canada for at least another year.

ACKNOWLEDGEMENTS

I am so thankful that God has given me the life I've had, and the ability to write about it. But I couldn't do it alone, so He provided a group of people who have faithfully helped me since my first book. Thank you so much for your various talents!

Maxine Isaac—You are always willing to listen and find avenues of possibilities for me.

Leola Kauffman—You are my sounding board when I need to vent.

Susan Miller—You both proofread and promote my books way down south.

Alice Vust—I can count on you to pick up the details I always miss.

Ralph and Helen Wiebe—You give me feedback to help me sharpen my skills.

I also want to thank my readers. Your willingness to buy my books to read enables me to continue to write. I pray this book will have been a blessing and an encouragement to you.

CPSIA information can be obtained
at www.ICGtesting.com
Printed in the USA
LVHW040934061122
732481LV00002B/221